Turn on the Power

How School is Limiting Your Child's Potential and What to Do About It

By Noel Jett, Ph.D., Haley Taylor Schlitz,
Nancy Shastid, and Myiesha Taylor M.D.

Gifted UNLIMITED

Edited by: Alexander Black, Type Right Editing
Interior design: The Printed Page
Cover design: Kelly Crimi

Published by
Gifted Unlimited, LLC
12340 U.S. Highway 42, No. 453
Goshen, KY 40026
www.giftedunlimitedllc.com

ISBN: 978-1-7337758-8-5

Printed and bound in the United States of America using partially recycled paper.

Contents

Prologue

Have you ever seen an outfit on a mannequin at a store and absolutely loved it? Then, when you tried it on, you were crushed because although it was advertised as one-size-fits-all, it simply won't fit? Maybe you bought it anyway? You kept thinking, "It just looked so good on the mannequin," neglecting to acknowledge the other half of the thought: "...but not on me." All too often, this is the reality of American K-12 education. The idea is wonderful, and you really want it to work, but for so many of us it simply does not.

One size never fits all.

Perhaps much more disturbing than the shopping example, have you ever watched a child lose interest in school right before your very eyes? Have you seen the face of the girl who is never called on, the boy who is punished for every infraction until he feels like he is being personally targeted, the students melting into their desks and waiting for the minutes to pass one second at a time? After growing up homeschooled, the first time I entered a public classroom as an adult irremovably burned a lyric from a Billy Joel song into my mind:

I see the children with their boredom and their vacant stares.
God help us all if we're to blame for their unanswered prayers.

Those of us lucky enough to have worked in middle schools have likely witnessed the turning point where motivated, friendly, creative students are finally beaten into submission by administration and even their fellow students, trading in academic passions for socially-acceptable time-wasting hobbies, seeking to blend in and shoot for the middle rather than accept themselves as they are and meet their maximum potential. There comes a time where girls become uncomfortable with math, where boys become uncomfortable with art, where everyone is just trying to survive one day at a time and balance interpersonal drama, a search for an identity, mandatory busywork, and whatever they may be experiencing at home: this all leaves little time for pursuit of what may have once been interesting and exciting for them in school. When you've seen a student being bullied by her own teacher for getting a question wrong, when you've seen a child beg not to be outed as the highest scorer on a test for the sake of their social standing, when you've seen the "crabs in a bucket" mentality make underprivileged students feel guilty for achieving, when you've seen a student who is working four grades ahead in every subject be told that they aren't ready to be accelerated…you've seen the exact moment that a part of that child's innocence is lost. Not every school is this bad, but even one is too many.

We offer this book to anyone who has ever experienced doubt or frustration dealing with the current U.S. educational system. If everyone this applied to bought our book, none of us would need to work ever again.

In the coming chapters, we will begin with some historical perspective on education in the US to show how we reached where we are today, we discuss the options available when public education is insufficient, and end with a reflection on the value of college. We also consider alternatives to the traditional K-12 scenario, which may well speed up the education process. We offer this book to reveal options you may not even be aware of as well as recounting the journeys of our two families. Our goal is to share those pathways to excellence and academic achievement that our traditional educational system may be unable to provide.

Our book incorporates facts, research, commentary, and deeply personal stories from two moms (one an M.D.) and their two daughters (one a Ph.D.). These personal stories are identified by author and come at the end of each chapter.

By the end of this book, we hope you will have found some wisdom, insight, laughter, and motivation to question the status quo. Most of all, our hope is that you will be able to turn on your power as parents and advocates for your children so they can reach their best potential.

About the authors:

Noel Jett, Ph.D.—was primarily homeschooled. She was a dual-enrolled student at Tarrant County Community College at age 13. She transferred to Texas A&M University at age 14 and graduated in 2015 at the age of 16 with a Bachelor of Science in Psychology. She immediately began her Ph.D. studies at the University of North Texas in Educational Psychology for the Gifted and Talented. She graduated with her Ph.D. in 2018 at the age of 19. She is now completing the requirements to become a Licensed Professional Counselor.

Haley Taylor Schlitz—attended public, private, and homeschool/hybrid schools before attending Tarrant County College at age 13. She graduated from Texas Women's University in 2019 at the age of 16 with a Bachelor of Science in Interdisciplinary Studies. She is currently a second-year law student at the Dedman School of Law at Southern Methodist University in Dallas.

Nancy Shastid—Noel's mom. Attended public schools in three states. By starting school a year early and attending summer school and night school, she skipped a year of high school and started college at the age of 16. She graduated from the University of Houston—Clear Lake with a B.S. in American Jurisprudence and had a career as a litigation paralegal before becoming a homeschool mom.

Myiesha Taylor, M.D.—Haley's mom. Graduated from Xavier University of Louisiana summa cum laude with a B.S. in Chemistry. She subsequently graduated with her medical degree from the University of Southern California School of Medicine and is now a homeschooling mom to Ian and Hana as well as a practicing physician.

Part 1
Establishing the Problem

CHAPTER 1
The Purpose of Public Education

Many of the disagreements about public education boil down to disagreements about the purpose of public education: Are we trying to create effective global citizens? Do we want to make kids smarter? Are we trying to promote equality by providing the same education to all Americans regardless of economic or racial background? Do we need to teach essential life skills? And, if we are not teaching these skills, is school really just babysitting?

To consider this, we must start at the beginning. To understand why American education exists as it does today, we must understand why it exists in the first place.

An authentic history of American education should, in fact, start with the educational practices of Native Americans. However, for our purposes, given the limited historical data available, we will begin with the first colonial settlements. The earliest accounts indicate that colonists hoped to mimic their own cultural traditions regarding education. English colonists were less interested in creating schoolhouses and more interested in using family, church, community, and apprenticeship as a means of raising and preparing children for adulthood, careers, and life skills. Math and reading, however, were taught at home by parents. With only rare exceptions, illiterate parents raised illiterate children. This was one of the biggest arguments for structured education; through education, we can advance beyond the class we were born into. The irony of this argument is that while at the time it claimed to be more egalitarian, the main beneficiaries were, in fact, white boys.

The Massachusetts Bay Colony was the first to criminalize truancy, making what they deemed "proper schooling" mandatory in 1642. Many types of education fell under this label, and they would include homeschooling, apprenticeship, and tutoring. Soon, the criminalization of truancy would become widespread in New England colonies.

The 18th century saw the popularization of "common schools" in which all students attended the same class with the same teacher regardless of their age. Although today we use different grades and classes, at the time common schools were still a step towards modern public education compared to the unstructured facilities of the 17th century. Another important aspect of these schools is that despite being mandatory, they were not free.

Some of the most important aspects of modern American education were established in the early 19th century. The freshly independent United States was hoping to establish its society and culture based on the concept of "Republican Motherhood," a philosophy fashioned by and for women which centered the success of society on family virtue. Therefore, theorists argued, women should be teachers as they understand children better and can pass along the morals and ethics Americans need. At the time, this successfully empowered women and led to increased access to education for girls.

By 1840, 55% of American children between the ages of five and fifteen attended primary schools or academies. The remaining children presumably came from families who could not afford tuition or to lose their free farmhands. It was around this time that schooling for girls beyond elementary education was introduced and girls' education began to more closely resemble that of boys. Until this point, girls were generally not taught math, science, or philosophy.

But wait a second. Girls usually only attended elementary school; they never learned math, science, or philosophy, so, what prepared women to be teachers? Nothing. Teachers were untrained and perhaps unskilled at that time, and hired mainly based on who they knew on the local school board and how low of a pay they could tolerate. The saying "those who can, do; those who can't, teach" may offend many today, but it was quite accurate at the time. There was also the fact that women were not legally permitted to "do" much of anything.

The dawn of the 20th century heralded a progressive new era for education and was a microcosm of the Progressive Movement throughout the West. If you have ever studied education, you likely know this was the time of John Dewey, a philosophy professor and a strong believer in the importance of democracy in education. This era led to an explosion of growth in the American educational system. Suddenly, schools were more common, served more children, and taught more subjects. While urban areas had always had the highest rates of school attendance, rural high schools also began to form in the 1900s. In 1880, high schools were thought of mainly as college preparation, and college was not yet a common goal. But by 1910, high schools had become a vital element of the common school system, preparing students for both college and vocations in the thriving industrial sector. By 1940, 50% of young adults earned a high school diploma. Remember, in 1840, only 55% of children attended primary school. This rapid progress is unparalleled in the history of education. This would also be the last time American education would be considered more effective than European education.

John Dewey believed that schooling was not just about teaching knowledge, but rather about teaching skills needed for active participation in a democratic society. While Republican Motherhood inspired moral teaching in school, the Progressive Movement inspired the teaching of life skills which lay somewhere between content and ethics.

And yet, while education and philosophy were thriving, equality was stagnant in the world of education. Girls were more educated but still unwanted in the workforce, just as they had been 100 years ago.

The work we women did do resembled less that of a 21st-century career and more that of a neighborhood saleswoman of Mary Kay or Tupperware. World War II was the inspiration for women to pursue careers, rather than any philosophical movement. As for non-white Americans, things were even worse; education was still segregated and still unequal. Booker T. Washington was perhaps the most influential black voice on issues of race in politics and education between 1890 and 1915. Although he advocated for increased quality of education in the black community in the South, his views were ultimately confined by the culture of the era in which he lived.

As the concept of public school became a more unified and popular idea, it took on familiar, modern-day characteristics that focused on discipline and rote memorization. Independent school districts depended on taxpayer money to fund and supervise public schools, as well as their capacity to design and implement their own system for educating and disciplining students. This was certainly a notable difference from the centralized systems prevalent in the rest of the Western world.

The Great Depression weakened America's public schools. Funding was reduced and teachers worked without pay for significant stretches of time. Roosevelt's New Deal was hardly sympathetic to this issue, refusing any requests for aid from public schools, private schools, or universities. However, New Deal relief programs did include the construction of new school buildings at the request of local governments.

Education under the New Deal was a total reversal of the advances of the progressive era, and indeed any theory of education based on the notion of "best practices." This is a fancy way of saying that before the Depression, people wanted school to reflect a certain degree of quality, and afterward, this desire apparently faded. New Deal schools returned to the practice of hiring underpaid and undereducated women as teachers, who in this case were essentially volunteer relief workers. Those progressive goals of creating skilled, professional students were abandoned and instruction became separated from any specific educational theory and the inspiration of education experts. New Deal education instead sought to be as anti elitist as possible. It was considered elitist to require educational credentials from teachers or to cater to any student who was not among the poorest or least privileged in society.

One could argue that today, the idea that teachers do not need to be licensed, or further the idea that schooling does not require a formal classroom setting, is more valid due to modern technology and the homeschooling movement. Contemporary research into formal teacher training and licensing has demonstrated that neither is strictly necessary for effective homeschooling from parents. However, in the case of the New Deal approach, this was a problem; that period predated many of the modern conveniences that supplement 21st-century education. Indeed, modern homeschooling is often more formal than New Deal public schooling; in many cases, it is also more scientific and is influenced by educational research. New Deal educational environments did not allow research-based influences, as the research itself was considered elitist at that time. Those of you familiar with the struggles of education for gifted students may perhaps appreciate the lasting effect which the New Deal approach left on our modern-day U.S. education.

During the 1930s, the budget and staff for the federal Office of Education were cut significantly. Alternatively, the Civilian Conservation Corps (CCC) was formed to offer free classes and opportunities to the uneducated. It was, however, specifically instructed to avoid teaching skills which would allow students to compete with unemployed union members. This is not necessarily a condemnation of the relief programs, as they were the administration's best plan to solve an extreme financial crisis and they did provide many benefits. For example, unemployed people were hired to construct or renovate public buildings which had an impact on 40,000 schools. While poor school districts were ignored, poor high school and college students were given scholarships and work-study opportunities.

The number of colleges in the United States skyrocketed in the early 20th century. In 1944, Congress passed the GI Bill which subsidized tuition and living expenses for veterans and offered a college education to those returning from service. The introduction of the GI Bill was the beginning of the societal perception of college as less of a luxury and more of a necessity. It also led to college campuses being mostly male, as only 2% of women were wartime veterans.

Passage of the Higher Education Act in 1965 provided federal scholarships and low-interest loans for college students. This allowed for the expansion and remodeling of existing colleges and created a demand for new institutions of higher learning. Later that year, the Elementary and Secondary Education Act passed, reallocating large sums of federal money to school districts.

The report "A Nation at Risk" was published in 1983 by the National Commission on Excellence in Education, condemning the way American schools held back those students with the highest potential. Although this report brought these issues to the attention of voters and politicians, even today there are still no mandates to support strong students anywhere near the extent of those advocating for weaker ones. Some people seem to feel that focusing on the smartest or highest achieving students means allowing less attention for those who appear to be less intuitive learners. Many new theories of education were either formed or popularized around this time, including "cultural literacy," which was a call to return our focus to the great ideas and classic works of the past, and specifically to teach students to decode and interpret them.

In the early 2000s, No Child Left Behind (NCLB) was introduced to thunderous applause. It was a popular, overwhelmingly bipartisan effort with many noble goals, including the goal that 100% of students would achieve a "proficient" level on standardized math and reading tests by 2014. We will get into how that turned out a bit later. This legislation punished schools for low performance on standardized tests. NCLB's goal was to serve struggling students the most, but because of its accountability-based funding allocations, underperforming schools, in fact, lost funding that would have benefited their weakest performing students. In many cases, NCLB also failed to serve high-achieving students; while high-performing schools continued to receive funding, learning outcomes for many gifted and high-achieving students remained unchanged. In 2015, a bipartisan Congress ended NCLB, replacing the federal education legislation with the Every Student Succeeds Act (ESSA).

Throughout the 2010s, requirements for cursive, recess, and the arts plummeted. Movements have formed to reinstate the arts and introduce skills such as computer science, teamwork, problem-solving, and analytic reasoning onto the syllabus. These latter skills are known as "21st-century skills," as they are intended to incorporate collaboration and critical thinking skills relevant to life and the workplace. Despite the addition of 21st-century skills to the school syllabus, public school curricula and learning dynamics have remained largely the same since the 1990s.

What does the history tell us?

Think back to the motivations for introducing public education as discussed at the beginning of the chapter. Does this sound like the story of a system designed to provide equitable education? In actual fact, we can be sure that public education was *not* designed to promote equality, as historically it has been segregated in almost every sense. An argument has recently been voiced that girls outperform boys in every first-world nation in every subject at every grade level because schools were designed to suit girls' strengths, thus giving them an unfair advantage. However, as we can see in the previous chapter, school was not even designed with girls in mind! Our earliest schools were male-only, and they stayed that way for a long, long time.

Trying to advocate for individual needs and differentiation in public school is a noble cause, but it is essentially a waste of time. Even if advocating for these things actually had any significant impact, it is like advocating for pizza to be served at Chipotle. Pizza is simply not what Chipotle was designed to serve. Individual needs are simply not what public school was designed to serve. Public education is produced for the masses, not tailored to the individual. This is no mistake; it's inherent to any public program.

In this chapter, we aimed to look at the history of public education to determine its ultimate purpose; the reason it was created in the first place. The truth is that there is likely no one perfect answer, and there is certainly no simple answer we can all agree on. But, if there is a story to be told, it is *not* one of equality...and as we move into the modern era, we may begin to anticipate how this story is not going to have a happy ending.

Measuring success (or a lack thereof) in modern-day schools

> *How do you measure a year?*
> *In daylights, in sunsets, in midnights, in cups of coffee?*
> *In inches, in miles, in laughter, in strife?*
> *525,600 minutes: How do you measure a year in the life?*

This is the riddle posed by *Seasons of Love* from the musical *Rent.* It's a good question and it exposes the main problem when it comes to any form of analysis: how do you measure anything? Measuring a year in 525,600 minutes is more accurate but it fails to truly capture the lived experiences of a year. The song ultimately proposes the alternative of measuring a year in love, which better captures the lived experience, but omits other aspects and is difficult to capture in any reliable way.

Measuring the effectiveness of different educational methods presents just as many conundrums, if not perhaps more. The only aspect of success the government is truly interested in is performance on standardized tests, which is unfortunately undermined by significant flaws in those tests, their importance when it comes to decisions on funding, and consequently the survival of any school that is preparing for the test. Thus, teaching to the test replaces all other forms of education.

The emotional, social, and psychological aspects of education are often considered less important than the academic aspects. Thus, the proverbial love is overshadowed by the proverbial minutes. We might ask ourselves at this point: If a medicine reduces the symptoms of an illness but has so many side effects that your quality of life does not improve, would you use it? Likewise, perhaps we should question the value of an educational practice that improves grades while impacting our social skills, life satisfaction, and/or extracurricular performance.

And isn't this how most of the school experience is ultimately justified? "Sure, it's boring, but it improves learning!" "Yeah it takes a long time, but it will make your grades better!" "You're not here to socialize, you're here to learn!"

As we have now seen, and will continue to explore in the coming chapters, what we are doing isn't necessarily rendering the results we expect. In the instances where desirable results are obtained, is it worth the price?

We offer a caveat to the data we will be presenting on education. Academic success is measured nearly exclusively by grades and achievement scores. Meaningful assessment of academic success extends beyond the impact of any given practice on grades. It is our position that such data provides an incomplete picture, and reveals that near exclusive priority is placed on performance and does not consider the "whole" student.

NCLB's goal was to raise all student achievement in mathematics and reading, with 100% of students scoring at proficient level by 2014. Unfortunately, it failed miserably. How miserably? In 2018, just 23% of Grade 12 students in American public schools were at or above proficient level in math, and only 36% met these standards in reading. If we now consider our high-achieving and gifted learners, just 10% of Grade 8 students were at or above the advanced level in math; this 10% is the highest score of any grade in any subject at this level. Sadly, the highest achievement in the teenage classroom is for 10% of students to reach the advanced level in math.

	Percentage of Students at *Advanced* Level or Higher		
Subject	**Grade 4**	**Grade 6**	**Grade 8**
Arts: Music	0	0	0
Arts: Visual Arts	0	0	0
Civics	1	2	4
Economics	0	0	3
Geography	1	3	1
Mathematics	8	10	2
Reading	9	4	6
Science	1	2	2
Technology & Engineering Literacy	0	3	0
U.S. History	2	1	1
Writing	2	3	3

Data from nationsreportcard.gov

"But wait," you say, "this study only represents public schools. Surely if we include non-public schools, the percentages will increase, as we all know that private and charter schools achieve higher scores." You're absolutely right; there is an increase when you account for non-public schools. The percentage of advanced geography students in fourth grade increases from 1% to a whopping (drumroll) 2%! That's it. No changes in any of the other subjects. It seems public education has a problem that private school isn't fixing.

It is important to note that private schools do not have to offer these exams, so we cannot include all private schools in these statistics. It's unclear what percentage of private schools are being included. The point is not to say that all private schools are marginally (or not at all) better than public schools, it is simply to illustrate that a private school is not inherently better for gifted learners, or any children, than a public school. This matters because there is a common misconception that sending a gifted kid to the nearest private school will solve all their issues when in reality, private schools vary widely. Parents need to vet schools before enrolling their children and consider the investment from a cost/benefit perspective.

"Yet surely our schools are outperforming other nations around the world!" you may retort, if you're one of those people who doesn't read the news. Let's consider the statistics: The World Top 20 Project gives ratings to education systems in different countries based on ten factors:

- early childhood enrollment rates for 3- to 4-year-olds
- primary completion for 6- to 11-year-olds
- lower secondary completion for 11- to 14-year-old
- high school graduation rates for 14- to 18-year-olds
- college graduation rates for 18- to 25-year-olds
- primary test scores for 6- to 11-year-olds
- lower secondary test scores for 11- to 14-year-olds
- school safety levels for 3- to 25-year-olds
- out-of-school children ages, 3- to 14-year-old
- adult illiteracy levels for 15-year-olds and up.

The US is not in the top 5 for any of these individually, nor the top 20 comprehensively. We ranked 26th in 2018, just ahead of Mexico and just behind Saudi Arabia. And according to the Progress in International Reading Literacy Study (PIRLS) 2016, neither was the United States in the top 10 countries for reading achievement (and just in case you are curious—out of 50 participating; girls outranked boys in 48 out of 50 countries).

There is, however, one general issue with comparing American education to that of other countries; it boils down to three main concerns. First, there are many ways to measure education and each has its own benefits and flaws. Second, collecting data is not as simple as asking countries to provide data, as many lack the infrastructure or even the honesty to provide quality data. Lastly, each country has its own unique culture, history, and current situation which means that comparing them is difficult. Singapore has consistently demonstrated that it has not only the most successful education system but also the most equitable: their ratio of low-SES (socioeconomic status) to high-SES students represented in their advanced education programs is only 1:2, for example—by comparison, America's is 1:34. Singapore is also one of the most rigid totalitarian governments in the first world (technically, it's a parliamentary constitutional republic, but chewing gum requires a permit). Singapore is also only a 30-minute drive from end to end (and that's the longest end), over 96.7% Asian (though this represents Chinese, Malay, and Indian populations, so there is certainly diversity), and home to under six million people. Singapore also has pretty disparate economic inequality, due less to a problem with poverty and more to a disproportionately rich section of the population (*Crazy Rich Asians*, anyone?). These people have more money than you can physically fit in the average house, so of course, they have every extracurricular educational resource money can buy.

So, is it really worth exploring the success of Singapore's education system? Absolutely, and we can certainly consider taking lessons from it to apply to US education; that seems appropriate. Let's just avoid getting our hopes up here.

Another repeat offender in the game of "we should be more like them; I saw a video about it on Facebook!" is Finland. Finland, unlike Singapore, *is* a country and has been so for more than 55 years (closer to 100, in fact). Finland's education system is famously adept at supporting gifted learners and produces creative, well-rounded students. Recess is mandatory, curricula are flexible, trade schools are thriving...and it's all included in the public system! In addition, they boast one of the highest rates of college degrees in the world. Yet they also have one of the highest rates of white people: Finland is 93% born Finnish. The remaining 7% tend to be from Russia, Estonia, and Sweden. But hey, no shame on white people, this book was written by two and a half white people. I just want to point out that educating a populace with a relatively unified cultural background is a simply not the reality of life in the United States. Similarly, Finland is also working with a 5.8% poverty rate as of 2018, while the U.S. is at least double that. Say what you will about the benefits of Finland's economic choices that have led to this lower poverty rate, at the end of the day, this is what we have to work with here. Educating someone who goes home to no dinner, or has no home to go home to, is incredibly difficult. Educating a populace with cultural backgrounds, priorities, and mother tongues as diverse as in America will always be a challenge.

The point is, there is more to improving education than simply borrowing ideas that seem to work in other countries. Beyond applicability issues, there is a cost as well. Even Asia's unrivaled educational success comes at a price: higher rates of teenage depression and suicide, for one, presumably due to the anxiety of underachievement. Our culture is neither better nor worse, just different. Adapting our public education system is a tediously difficult, slow, and controversial process. Adapting our nationwide culture is presumably near impossible. This is a major motivation for why we will be promoting homeschooling throughout this book: when you are in control of your education, you can incorporate many of these positive and beneficial global influences into the lives of your children in a way the public system cannot, and you can do so much more quickly. As a homeschooler or hybrid educator of any kind, you can make recess mandatory tomorrow if you want!

If the practices indicated to be most effective had been implemented over the past half century, we would not recognize our public education classrooms today. In fact, studies suggest that public education's principal practices are demonstrably unproductive (if not harmful) at almost every turn.

Current practices	Recommendations from recent research
Large classrooms	Smaller classrooms are typically better, especially for students who are performing poorly in larger classrooms (Blatchford, Bassett, & Brown, 2011; NICHD, 2004)
Kids must be silent and sit still	Kids who are able to move freely remember content better (Carson, Shih, & Langer, 2001). Research in cognition and memory has consistently found that attention is held by changing stimuli rather than focusing on one thing: children learn better when they can get up and move around and see things from multiple perspectives than if they must stay still and stare at the same thing (Pavlov, 1927; Phaf & Wolters, 1993).

Arts programs are being cut (Amrein-Beardsley, 2009; Tambucci, 2006)	Art programs improve student achievement and train higher-order thinking skills (Gullatt, 2007; Hetland & Winner, 2001), as well as stimulating student motivation, student engagement, development of executive functioning skills, and development of social skills (Christine, 2011). Music instruction specifically benefits spatial and temporal reasoning (Črnčec, Wilson, & Prior, 2006).
Recess time is shorter overall and removed as punishment (Pellegrini, 2005)	Recess improves children's cognitive performance (Pellegrini & Bjorklund, 2010; Pellegrini & Bohn, 2005) and classroom behavior (Barros, Silver, & Stein, 2009). Additionally, researchers have observed numerous physical and mental health benefits of active physical play and being outdoors (McKenzie & Kahan, 2008; Janssen & LeBlanc, 2010; Biddle & Asare, 2011; Boreham & Riddoch, 2010; Biddle, Gorely, & Stensel, 2004; Gladwell, Brown, Wood, Sandercock, & Barton, 2013; Larson, Green, & Cordell, 2011; Ulset et al., 2017; Beyer, Szabo, & Nattinger, 2016)
All students taught the same information in the same style	Differentiation has been found to help all students achieve, but it is difficult to implement due to "teaching to the test" and the sheer number of students with differing needs in the same class.
Testing relies mainly on ability to read, write, and speak English	This practice discriminates against linguistically and culturally diverse students as well as students with learning disabilities, and non-verbal alternative testing is not always offered or measures the same concepts effectively.
Homework is assigned to all ages, and students may spend upwards of two hours a night on it	Homework does not improve grades or standardized test scores in elementary students, barely improves performance in middle school, and is not useful in high school when exceeding two hours a night (Cooper, Robinson, & Patall, 2006).

Sometimes, when advocating for the value of homeschool or otherwise family-controlled education over government-controlled efforts, we may be accused of not caring about public schools: "Some kids need them, some kids benefit from them, but some families will never be able to offer their children homeschool or private school or charter school or online school!" Yes, this is all true. Yet advocating for homeschooling and advocating for the betterment of public schools are in no sense mutually exclusive. Of course, we realize and acknowledge the importance of having an educated society. But perhaps we might consider our argument akin to advocating for individualization of a treatment plan for an individual patient which places their specific personal issues at the forefront. What is good for a population may be detrimental to an individual patient. For instance, the U.S. Preventive Services Task Force recommends screening mammograms for women aged 50-74 years old. However, if the individual woman has a personal history or a family history of breast cancer, her screenings should begin decades beforehand. As such, the recommendation for the masses may benefit *most* people (which is the purpose of screening and public health recommendations); however, it is important to consider the unique circumstances of the individual human being when recommending courses of action.

What we've seen in this chapter is how expectations compare to the reality of American education, not just in terms of statistics but framed within the historical context that hopefully can help us appreciate *why* we're in the position that we are now. Looking forward, we have to take into account what practices actually benefit children the most on an individual level before we can even begin to change what is currently being done.

In conclusion, public programs provide amazing opportunities and yet come with inherent flaws. Another example of this might include public television: it provides the essential programming needs of any family (news, weather, children's entertainment) for "free" through taxpayer funds to anyone with a television and bunny ear antenna. Public television is great, most people like it, most people want to see it thrive and prosper. And yet, you'd probably pay for cable. Or Netflix, or Hulu, or Vudu, or Amazon Prime, YouTube TV, Redbox rentals and the like, or perhaps you'd prefer a selection of the above services. Public television isn't enough to meet the entirety of your entertainment needs, so you spend the money you've earned on things that help you enjoy your life. Why shouldn't you? Does this mean that you don't care about public television, or that you wish it didn't exist? Does it mean you look down on those who only watch that and nothing else? Obviously not. If you're willing to put time, money, and energy into additional resources for your entertainment even though there is decent stuff available for free, why wouldn't you do the same for your child's education?

Despite the rhetoric and the chorus of opinions, the numbers don't lie. Public education, like public television, simply isn't enough for a significant portion of the populace.

References

Altschuler, G. & Blumin, S. (2009). *The GI Bill: The new deal for veterans.* Oxford University Press.

Amrein-Beardsley, A. (2009). Twilight in the valley of the sun: Nonprofit arts and culture programs in Arizona's public schools post-No Child Left Behind. *Arts Education Policy Review, 110*(3). https://doi.org/10.3200/AEPR.110.3.9-17

"Archived: Fact Sheet on No Child Left Behind." U.S. Department of Education.

Barros, R. M., Silver, E. J., & Stein, R. E. K. (2009). School recess and group classroom behavior. *Pediatrics, 123*(2), 431-436. https://doi.org/10.1542/peds.2007-2825

Bernstein, I. (1996). *Guns or Butter: The Presidency of Lyndon Johnson.* Oxford University Press. pp. 202–222. ISBN 0-19-506312-0.

Beyer, K. M. M., Szabo, A., Nattinger, A. B. (2016). Time spent outdoors, depressive symptoms, and variation by race and ethnicity. *American Journal of Preventive Medicine, 51*(3), 281-290. https://doi.org/10.1016/j.amepre.2016.05.004

Biddle, S. J. H. & Asare, M. (2011). Physical activity and mental health in children and adolescents: A review of reviews. *British Journal of Sports Medicine, 45*, 886-895.

Biddle, S. J. H., Gorely, T. & Stensel, D. J. (2004). Health-enhancing physical activity and sedentary behaviour in children and adolescents. *Journal of Sports Sciences, 22*(8), 679-701. https://doi.org/10.1080/02640410410001712412

Blatchford, P., Bassett, P., & Brown, P. (2011). Examining the effect of class size on classroom engagement and teacher–pupil interaction: Differences in relation to pupil prior attainment and primary vs. secondary schools. *Learning and Instruction, 21*(6), 715-730. https://doi.org/10.1016/j.learninstruc.2011.04.001

Boreham, C. & Riddoch, C. (2001). The physical activity, fitness and health of children. *Journal of Sports Sciences, 19*(12), 915-929. https://doi.org/10.1080/026404101317108426

Bower, K. P. "'A favored child of the state': Federal Student Aid at Ohio Colleges and Universities, 1934–1943." *History of Education Quarterly* 44.3 (2004): 364-387.

Brill, S. (2011). *Class warfare: Inside the fight to fix America's schools.* Simon and Schuster.

Carson, S., Shih, M., & Langer, E. (2001). Sit Still and Pay Attention? *Journal of Adult Development, 8*(3), 183-188. https://doi.org/10.1023/A:1009594324594

Cooper, H., Robsinson, J. C., Patall, E. A. (2006). Does homework improve academic achievement? A synthesis of research, 1987-2003. *Review of Educational Research, 76*(1), 1–62. https://doi.org/10.3102/00346543076001001

Cremin, L. (1970). *American education: The colonial experience, 1607–1783.* City: Harper & Row.

Črnčec, R., Wilson, S. J., Prior, M. (2006). The cognitive and academic benefits of music to children: Facts and fiction. *Educational Psychology, 26*(4), 579-594. https://doi.org/10.1080/01443410500342542

Dwyer, M. C. (2011). Reinvesting in arts education: Winning America's future through creative schools. President's Committee on the Arts and the Humanities.

1840 Census Data. *Progress of the United States in Population and Wealth in Fifty Years*, accessed February 11th, 2019.

Generals, D. (2000). Booker T. Washington and Progressive Education: An experimentalist approach to curriculum development and reform. *Journal of Negro Education, 69*(3), 215–234.

Gladwell, V. F., Brown, D. K., Wood, C., Sandercock, G. R., & Barton, J. L. (2013). The great outdoors: How a green exercise environment can benefit all. *Extreme Physiology & Medicine, 2*(3). https://doi.org/10.1186/2046-7648-2-3

Goldin, C. & Katz, L. F. (2008). *The Race between Education and Technology.* Cambridge: Belknap Press of Harvard University Press. ISBN 978-0-674-02867-8.

Gullatt, D. E. (2007). Research links the arts with student academic gain. *The Educational Forum, 71*(3), 211-220. https://doi.org/10.1080/00131720709335006

Herbst, J. *The Once and Future School: Three Hundred and Fifty Years of American Secondary Education* (1996)

Hetland, L. & Winner, E. (2001). The arts and academic achievement: What the evidence shows. *Arts Education Policy Review, 102*(5), 3-6. https://doi.org/10.1080/10632910109600008

Janssen, I. & LeBlanc, A. G. (2010). Systematic review of the health benefits of physical activity and fitness in school-aged children and youth. *International Journal of Behavioral Nutrition and Physical Activity, 7*(40). https://doi.org/10.1186/1479-5868-7-40

Larson, L. R., Green, G. T., & Cordell, H. K. (2011). Children's time outdoors: Results and implications of the National Kids Survey. *Journal of Park and Recreation Administration, 29*(2), 1-20.

McKenzie, T. L. & Kahan, D. (2008). Physical activity, public health, and elementary schools. *The Elementary School Journal, 108*(3), 171-180. https://doi.org/10.1086/529100

Nelson, A. R. & Rudolph, J. L. (2010). *Education and the Culture of Print in Modern America.* p. 160.

NICHD Early Child Care Research Network. (2004). Does class size in first grade relate to children's academic and social performance or observed classroom processes? *Developmental Psychology, 40*(5), 651-664. http://dx.doi.org/10.1037/0012-1649.40.5.651

Parkerson, F., Parkerson, D. H., & Parkerson, J. (2001) *Transitions in American Education: A Social History of Teaching.* Routledge. Ch 1.

Pavlov, I. P. (1927). *Conditioned reflexes: An investigation of the physiological activity of the cerebral cortex.* London: Oxford University Press.

Pellegrini, A. D. (2005). *Recess: Its role in education and development.* Psychology Press.

Pellegrini, A. D. & Bohn, C. M. (2005). The role of recess in children's cognitive performance and school adjustment. *Educational Researcher, 34*(1), 13-19. https://doi.org/10.3102/0013189X034001013

Phaf, R. H., &Wolters, G. (1993). Attentional shifts in maintenance rehearsal. *American Journal of Psychology, 106*(3), 353-382.

Reese, W. J. (2001). The origins of progressive education. *History of Education Quarterly, 41*(1), 1–24.

Rhodes, J. (2012). *An education in politics: The origins and evolution of No Child Left Behind.* Cornell U.P. pp. 179–81.

Rousmaniere, K. (2013). *The principal's office: A social history of the American school principal.* State University of New York Press. ISBN 978-1-4384-4823-7.

"Schooling, Education, and Literacy, In Colonial America." faculty.mdc.edu. 2010-04-01. Archived from the original on 2011-01-10.

Tambucci, S. (2006) The promise of arts education. *American School Board Journal,193*(6). 34–35

Tyack, D., Lowe, R., & Hansot, E. (1984). *Public schools in hard times: The Great Depression and recent years.* Cambridge, Massachusetts: Harvard University Press.

Ulset, V., Vitaro, F., Brendgen, M., Bekkhus, M., Borge, A. I. H. (2017). Time spent outdoors during preschool: Links with children's cognitive and behavioral development. *Journal of Environmental Psychology, 52*, 69-80. https://doi.org/10.1016/j.jenvp.2017.05.007

"U.S. spending." *Rolling Stone.* April 19, 1990. p. 43.

Veysey, L. R. (1965). *The Emergence of the American University.* Chicago: University of Chicago Press.

Looking Back with Nancy: Kindergarten Drop-Out

Life in a master-planned community in north Fort Worth offered the illusion of luscious parks, landscaped esplanades, and lovely schools for our little angel to attend, even if we did live in one of the smallest homes.

As the spring of 2003 came into blossom, so came the time for the Kindergarten Roundup, as they call it down here in the South. Our lovely neighborhood school, Bluebonnet Elementary, was ready for a headcount of incoming Kindergarteners. Thus, we joined the herd, made our way to school, and jumped in line for the cattle call. Knowing that my little darling already seemed to skew bright, I planned to be a helpful yet squeaky wheel to assure that her needs were met; think, Volunteer of the Year, PTA President, etc. But honestly, I planned to be involved no matter what.

Back in those days, we could choose morning or afternoon Kindergarten, as three hours a day was all that was deemed necessary. Although surveys showed that parents wanted full-day kindergarten and the private schools that offered such had waiting lists, I was more than happy about the way things were, as I thought 3 hours a day of Kindergarten was sufficient. We chose afternoons, and our easy mornings remained the same.

As it turned out, our humble abode was exactly 2.1 miles from the school and thus qualified for bus service. It felt as if we were in a small, country town, not a part of the Dallas/Fort Worth metropolis, when that little yellow school bus came right up to our house and honked its horn. There were only 3 kids on that route, one of which was a neighbor friend across the way. It was an easy and comfortable routine of skipping down the driveway each day at noon.

The ride home, however, was on the big bus with kids as old as fourth graders. We reluctantly tried that once. News flash: turns out that older kids will be mean to little kids sometimes. That was a no-go from then on. I preferred to pick my daughter up anyway and to get the low-down on the day's events while they were still fresh.

But then I had a new problem: I was not getting a lot of details from my otherwise talkative princess. She was happy enough, but either there wasn't much to report or there was something sinister afoot—at least, that was what my slightly paranoid-self suspected. I had long since turned in the paperwork to be a classroom volunteer, and after waiting longer than seemed reasonable, I straight-up lied to the teacher and told her that my background check had come through—I was there to volunteer. She was surprised at the fast turnaround, but happier to ask for forgiveness than permission, I was able to use a big smile and a confident countenance to get my foot in the door (and no, I didn't even kind of feel bad about it).

The classroom was well-designed, adorably decorated, fun, colorful, and engaging. The teacher was experienced and pleasant. Observing the classroom in action, however, was painful. From my non-teacher point of view, the pace was excruciatingly slow and content overwhelmingly uninteresting. I watched as the adorable 5 and 6-year olds scurried to sit on the slightly elevated stage area of the classroom, either near their friends or near the teacher in her rocking chair. My adorable princess seemed to settle in easily enough, although a couple of boys were clamoring to sit next to her. The teacher pulled out a book and pointed to the large letter "L" and then used her arm to make the motions to demonstrate a giant "L." It was then that I noticed Noel start to look about the room and the occasional jostling of the boys next to her. I saw her eventually look back to the teacher, but as soon as she realized that she was still making the "L" sound and using her arm to motion the letter again, she returned to scanning the room.

It was at that moment that I began to see myself in her. Picture me at conferences, which I was paid to attend and for which the expenses were covered by my employer. I am a professional needing continuing legal education credits to maintain my national certification, and I too begin to scan the room for something more interesting when the speaker starts stating things I sort of already knew. I would make a grocery list, think of old friends I should check on, and do anything but give my full attention. I was mortified for her, and quite embarrassed for myself as well.

It then came time for the classroom to be broken up into smaller groups to go to "centers." The twenty-one students were divided up into various clusters for a myriad of educational activities. Four students were told to work with me. As assignments were given, I watched the kids go to their assigned places. I was still a bit confused as to what they were to do at each center, as no additional information was given. Noel and Connor were assigned to the "color center." I did not know what that meant and it was in a nook of the classroom that I could not directly see. I kid you not, not one iota, that the teacher said no less than *five times* to my child: "Noel, don't help Connor." "Okay sweetie, don't help Connor." "Noel, don't help." "Got it, Noel? Don't help Connor." I was baffled. What in the world is up with Connor and this mysterious color center? But off the two went to engage in this elusive and seemingly complex operation.

In the meantime, I was given four students to work with on letter recognition. I was given a small case with old-school hexagonal wooden blocks with a letter on each side. I was sure this must be far below par as a lesson for kindergarteners in a "good school" and a "good neighborhood", but what did I know compared to this experienced teacher? I assumed that the exercise might be to remind them of the difference between "p" and "q" or between "b" and "d." Maybe she was trying to give them an easy "win" with a simple exercise or perhaps to keep me busy. I quickly discovered that this was neither. The students could not recognize the letters. I was simply stunned. Had the teacher given me the four slowest kids in the class? Had they never watched Sesame Street? How can you not know the Letter of the Day? My mind slowly opened up to realize the obvious—kids simply learn at different speeds.

As I shook off the shock, I reminded myself that I needed to see what this elusive "color center" was all about. As I turned the corner, I saw a laminated poster of colorful crayons with names of each color easily readable in bold print. Noel and Connor had a multi-page, black and white printout with various shapes and names of colors printed inside of each shape. For example, there was a circle with "pink" written in the middle, and a triangle with the word "red." The task is to color in the shape with the appropriate color. Ahh, okay, got it. Color center. I watched Noel color as instructed. Not too interesting, but sure. Young Mr. Connor then asked me in the most incredulous tone for a dude pushing six, "Can she really read?" As I look to Connor to answer his question, I see he is coloring in that "red" triangle with a purple crayon, and I stumble for a reply. I didn't want to make Connor feel bad, yet I didn't want to diminish the achievements of my daughter. Perhaps teaching her to hide her talents to make others feel less intimidated, is, at best, a mediocre parenting move. So, I hedged and said, "She can read a little." Connor responded with a defiant "I can too!" I replied "Awesome!" I never considered jealousy, judgment, teacher intonation, the appropriate responses to frustrated five-year-olds, the boredom, or the million other issues kindergarten was introducing. I just assumed that kindergarten in my lovely neighborhood would be, well, lovely. And if it needed tweaking, I would help make that work. But just as a broken arm needs more than a band-aid, there was way more needed than mere tweaking.

I have forever been befuddled by Connor's question and his accompanying statement. What was my five-year-old supposed to do with that? Did he ask for help that day, or maybe in the past? Did Noel say yes or no? Did she obey the teacher and thus disobey my parenting mantra of always being helpful? Did she "cheat" and subvert authority by helping Connor? Did she ignore him? How are any of the above options a good choice? How did Connor manage all this? Did he know he cannot read? Will he be mean to her because she can? I was worried about middle school in the future. Who knew the politics of kindergarten could be so complex!

My foray into volunteering left me more than befuddled. No wonder Noel had so little to say: there wasn't much to report, at least nothing of any interest. I had raised her to be polite. Aren't all little future Southern Belles supposed to be polite? She wouldn't think to complain much, as she had been so excited at the thought of attending school. All her friends were, too. But I could see the cogs in her head begin to turn. I saw the future like a montage from a movie. I saw her becoming the teacher's pet, little miss know-it-all with no friends, or little miss help-everyone-else and learn nothing yourself, or perhaps starting to notice those boys wanting to sit next to her and stop noticing anything else... Or perhaps worst of all, dumbing down just to fit in. Shock turned into action.

It occurred to me that I needed to have Noel tested to determine if she really was way ahead of the class. I knew nothing whatsoever about testing a 5-year-old and lest I be seen as obnoxious, I chose not to ask around much either. I relied on a casual comment from a psychologist and booked an appointment with a pricey educational diagnostician who performed a full IQ and achievement testing. It turned out that there were many more affordable options that I could have taken advantage of to get the information that I needed. But, alas, I was still shell-shocked from the volunteering experience and wanted to get information as quickly as possible.

Despite the expense, that report changed our trajectory in an amazing, life-changing way. I am so much more than $800 thankful! Noel had a fun time doing puzzles and answering questions and I had a full report that told me that she was above grade level by every measure, and extraordinarily so on many. But mostly, I had the words of this lovely older woman with a Ph.D. at the end of her name tell me that I needed to homeschool. She said that Noel had an innate love of learning and that "school will kill her." Wait, what! Kill her? This Ph.D. elaborated that some private schools will try to group smarter kids together, but even that accommodation would not likely work. She said Noel would be better suited to homeschooling. I was stunned, confused, more enlightened, yet unsure.

I took the report to the school principal and he said that there was no one at the school as smart as her. He offered to move her to a morning kindergarten class as there was one kid who was ahead like her, just not as much. Or maybe he could move her to first grade for reading. But we liked afternoon kindergarten, and she needed more than first grade for reading. And, and, and...now I was starting to get it. She would likely always be odd-man-out for minimal return. She would have to endure constant change to fit in, which would probably never even be enough anyways. She would be bored to tears or pushed too hard, alongside a million other experiences that would never be to her advantage. I suddenly understood why the Ph.D. had said school would kill her love of learning, and potentially kill *her*. That $800 was becoming more and more valuable.

In the meantime, the teacher did (at my request) give her some moderately appropriate work to do. Sadly, she ended up giving it as homework…isn't that a bit much for a 5-year-old? She was to read a chapter of any of her books at night, draw a picture, and write a sentence or two about it. Easy peasy! The teacher would check her folder during the day and give her a cutesy sticker of some kind and write "good job" or "great" or some other affirmation. It seemed like a step forward, albeit a baby step. But then the teacher stopped. I checked her folder daily to see what info or announcements were sent home, yet the homework stopped getting checked. Well, that isn't very nice. Did the teacher forget? Was she too busy? Didn't care? Resentful of more work? I never knew. Regardless, I was left supervising the "home" work of my 5-year-old and giving her the affirmation that the teacher does not. So, I am acting like a teacher, in my home. Hmm…cue the foreshadowing music.

I nonetheless waited for the official parent-teacher conference at the end of nine weeks of our half-day Kindergarten. I was hoping they would have figured out what should be done to educate my daughter. They were the professionals. They had the pretty school with the pretty name and the pretty everything, which included the pretty mantra, "We take them where they are and move them forward." I truly, earnestly asked how does one do that when my kid is reading chapter books and these kids don't know their letters? The mantra was repeated. Platitudes offered. A plan? Well, none really. It was a hard "no" from me, but "thanks" for trying. I withdrew her. Kindergarten drop out: whatever would become of her?

Looking Back with Myiesha: About Public School

Hana, my youngest child, was eager to go to public school. We live in a very good district, in fact, having bought our house because of the feeder pathway into the local high school. Haley graduated from this elementary school, our son Ian attended for two years: we had had great experiences!

But, once Haley got to the intermediate school, we opted to homeschool. That meant Hana never got to experience a public, or in any way traditional, school.

She desperately wanted to try it; she'd been asking for two years! "Can I go to school every day?" "Can I have a locker like Haley did?" "Can I pick out a lunchbox?" How can you say no to a little girl *begging* to go to school? She came from Ethiopia where her access to school was so limited, which made it even tougher to turn her down. So, we signed her up.

Initially, things were fantastic. She loved everything about public school—from picking her outfits each day to interacting with teachers to learning new things. Every single day, she looked forward to going back.

A few weeks into the semester I asked her, "What are you learning?"

"Well, we're starting to do practice STAAR tests. I think I did okay," she tells me.

I had honestly forgotten about standardized testing. Clearly, I had gotten used to the freedom of homeschooling.

I asked her about her classmates. She responded that "no one really plays with me. I know one girl, but she doesn't behave well, and you told me not to get in trouble hanging around bad kids." I ask her who she sits next to in the cafeteria (because, <sarcasm font> we need them to socialize, right? </sarcasm font>). She says that she has to sit in a line with her class, and, shockingly, she adds that she wishes she could sit alone.

"Why?" I ask. "Are they making you feel excluded? You are easily *the* most social person I know! You love people! Why are you saying you'd rather be alone?"

Hana responds, "I think it's just because I don't know anyone except one girl on my table." I tell her that I know it's hard at first, but I'm sure that it'll get better. You go to school to learn, not to make friends. Over time, Hana seemed to integrate nicely into the class, and the teacher was very communicative with us as parents. However, gradually the enthusiasm and optimism waned.

Over the coming months, I become more concerned that these issues are taking a psychological toll, but she insisted that everything was fine. I conscripted Haley to talk to her (because sometimes you need a sister, not a mom), and it became apparent that everything was, in fact, not at all fine. The girls at school were quintessential "mean girls" and Hana didn't fit in. When she asked to join their social circle, she was told that she wasn't really American and that she was going to be "sent back to Africa where she came from." When another girl spoke up on her behalf, refuting that statement, the mob quickly turned on her as well by questioning her immigration status. Both girls were silenced. Hana was hurt, because obviously, this would hurt anyone. She was increasingly unhappy with her entire situation and felt that nobody liked her. She ate lunch alone, or with a couple of boys. That worked to lessen the loneliness, until the other girls got jealous because one of them had a crush on one of the boys; the mean girl clique tightened its squeeze on Hana.

Not too long later, Hana was hit on the head with a stick at school by one of the boys—her "best friend," apparently, because he's the only one that will sit with her at lunch. He says it was an accident; Hana's doctor says she has a concussion. She's pulled out of school for four days, with no P.E. for a week thereafter. For days after returning to school, Hana goes to the nurse's office multiple times complaining of various ailments in an effort to be sent home.

When I casually offer that she could always come back and homeschool, she's more excited than she's ever been to do it. She instantly accepts, and we pull her out.

When you have a plant being watered with acid, it's much easier, or at least significantly more effective, to stop watering with acid and provide fresh water than to try to neutralize the acid by adding additional chemicals. Home is fresh water. In this situation, every other option simply felt like adding more chemicals.

People tend to talk about public school through the lens of their own anecdotal experience. If you live in certain areas, in some states, in a "good" neighborhood, with the right economic resources, your experience may be great. The problem comes when we take our own personal experience and project it on public schools across the nation. Public schools a few blocks away from each other can be fundamentally different;

extrapolate that across state lines and you can see that an accurate discussion of public school as one unified, generalized entity is simply not possible.

If you can also factor in issues around race/ethnicity and gender, then you may see how the experiences of a young white male student could be different than that of an African-American female student in the exact same class. Even in a great neighborhood with a great school, you're not safe from the world. It may sound obvious, but when your child gets told by a classmate that they are going to be sent back to Africa, you realize you'll never be wholly prepared for the harsh reality of how cruel people, even little kids, can be. We complained and nothing was done to address it. There was not even an apology. (Although, to be honest, how much could a half-hearted, forced apology from a child really do, when we all know they're going to continue to repeat whatever they hear at home?) As great as our local elementary school was in so many ways, our youngest daughter Hana was being mistreated. It was painful as a parent to admit that I couldn't fix it. Homeschooling doesn't fix sexism or racism either, but it helps you introduce your child to certain topics at a slightly slower and more personalized basis, with the comfort of family support. It also helps you introduce your child to other topics at an earlier stage, hence why it is so beneficial for fast learners. When you actually have control over your child's socialization and community, rather than just throwing them in the deep end with whoever happens to live nearby with limited (if not actively mediocre) adult supervision, you also gain control over how to handle these situations as a parent.

The American public school system is failing millions of children from all backgrounds, not necessarily because people don't care, but because there are inherent, implicit biases that are incredibly difficult to address. Teachers and administrators, even if they mean well, are often unable to move beyond unconsciously accepted stereotypes and beliefs. It's not a white problem or a male problem, people of all races and gender subconsciously believe in and actively reinforce stereotypes, even stereotypes of their own race and gender. Most teachers are women, but if being a woman meant not being sexist, there would be significantly fewer people experiencing sexism in school. Hell, if being a woman meant not being sexist, sexism would be less of a global issue overall because women have outnumbered men throughout many points in history. Hana's bullying at the hands of the mean girls because of her affiliation with a boy that one of them crushed on is a great example of how oppressed people will gladly attack their own for the approval of the oppressors.

What made homeschooling work so well for us was a strong sense of commitment: we went all in. We owned it because we had to. We accepted that the convenience and simplicity of public school were outweighed by the danger it brought. We had to provide an education to our children and do our best not to screw it up.

Chapter 2
How Children Learn

Perhaps the biggest downside of traditional education is that a large group of children is expected to all learn the same way: they will receive the same lecture, the same assignments, and at the end, all be judged equally rather than equitably. It is of particular note that the way these children are taught is *not* informed by research about how children learn best, or by parent input on how their child can be engaged; it is rarely even informed by the teacher's own opinions based on their experience with hundreds of kids. As is often mentioned in discussions about the typical classroom format and it's failings, "if you judge a fish by its ability to climb a tree, it will live its whole life believing that it is stupid." What if I told you the proverbial monkeys of the classroom, the kids who do the best because everything is built for their skill set, are not always the smartest kids in the class? They're just the best climbers! The worst aspect of this is that many kids with astonishing skills in other areas are forced to abandon their passion and talent in favor of tree-climbing.

If you take time to re-evaluate how your child learns best, you may gain some fascinating new insights into their preferred learning environment. Take a minute to forget everything you know about education: forget how school works, forget what you were taught about how to teach, just erase it. If you had never seen a schoolroom before in your life, would you decide to have each student sit in an individual plastic chair with a wooden desk, arranged in rows and columns? Try to justify that decision *without* referencing its ubiquity, prove that it is a good system based solely on its merit. You're probably realizing there are no obvious reasons to arrange schoolrooms in this way. Now think of a classroom with couches, bean bags, rugs, rocking chairs, pillows…you're probably thinking "well, wouldn't that distract the students?"

No. That's not the point. Would that distract *your* student? Now you're thinking about your family's needs, something that was not done when the traditional school system was designed.

When we start again from scratch, we can customize in ways we hadn't even considered before. Kids tend to prefer to move around and be physically active, and this can actually help them learn rather than distract from it. The reality is that there are a plethora of ways to teach different students based on their own intellectual level, pace of learning, and how they learn best.

It can be difficult to determine a learner's preferred learning conditions. One person's parameters for how to learn best are not always self-evident, either to you or your teacher, and in any case a classroom teacher can hardly accommodate her lessons to the needs of every student. It can be especially hard to determine the learning needs of a student who is not a native English speaker. Communication barriers are hard to get past and can even result in gifted students being put in a special needs class. One of the beauties of homeschooling is that you have the time to go through the trial and error process of finding what works best with your student. A defining and universal feature in every learning experience is a sense of success to maintain motivation: hitting a brick wall because a certain learning style is too difficult can be easily rectified through the flexibility afforded through homeschooling.

Playing to each child's individual interests and strengths is an easy way to keep them motivated and help them excel. Many gifted kids become so focused on their topic of choice or preferred future career that they lose interest in other topics ("I know I'm going to be a doctor, so why do I need to learn history?"). There are a few ways you can go with this. Many educational advocates feel that the "jack of all trades" approach to education goes on for too long and that we should allow students to explore their passions and talents sooner (this is a common element of the Talent Development paradigm of gifted education). If you agree with your kid that history is gravy, we see the merit in letting them just get the basics down and then spending more time developing what they're actually good at and enjoy. If not, you can make use of interdisciplinary work in a way public schools rarely have the chance to. These are *just a few* of the ways you could integrate multiple topics to synthesize learning for your student:

- Science and Government/Law: How do the system of a cell (mitochondria, endoplasmic reticulum, phospholipid layer) or the systems of the body (endocrine system, nervous system, respiratory system) compare to systems of government (judiciary system, congress, executive, and even services like police and fire departments)?
- Psychology and History: Consider the thinking patterns and personalities of historical figures and their decisions. What motivates leaders to take control? What beliefs lie behind differing political movements? What could make someone become a horrific dictator like Mao or Stalin?
- Math and Art: What makes certain paintings aesthetically pleasing? How does mathematics affect other visual mediums (i.e. design, architecture, photography)? How do mathematical principles like the Golden Ratio and the Fibonacci sequence play out in art over the centuries?
- Foreign Language, Social Studies, Linguistics, Geography, and World History: Map the history of a language across the globe, noting how it changed in terms of physical relocation and impact on culture. A brief example might be how Spanish originated in Latin which was spoken in the Roman Empire which encompassed huge portions of Europe. Celtic, Greek, and Arabic influences are of note. Castilian Spanish, as spoken today mainly by the elite classes of Spain,

is influenced by Mozarabic, a dead language once used by Christians in medieval Spain under Islamic rule. By the twentieth century, British English lent many Anglican terms and patterns to Spanish, and Spain began conquering the Native Americans of Central and South America. Today, Spain and its former colonies share a language but have unique dialects and cultures (for example, the "s" sound is often spoken in a lisped "th" sound in Spain, while in most Latin American countries it is pronounced as an "s").

- Physics and Home Economics (in this case, cooking): What properties of heat transfer and thermodynamics take place when a steak is first seared on the pan and then baked in the oven? The goal of this process is to preserve the moisture inside the meat, but why does it work? Many people add salt to their water when cooking pasta: should the salt be added before or after the water is boiling, and why? Boil two pots of a green vegetable and add divalent salt to one of them. After cooking for just a few minutes, the salted vegetables will be a brighter green color...why is this? Why does water boil at a lower temperature at higher altitudes? You could even throw in some Geography: mark some points on the map of varying altitude and calculate how long it would take to cook the perfect hard-boiled egg in each location based on the differing atmospheric pressure.
- Chemistry and Statistics: Create a hypothesis relating to chemical interactions, and use the scientific method to figure out how to explore this hypothesis. Conduct several instances of this experiment with a control and a testing group. Use the results to conduct a quantitative analysis: what percentage of the test group produced the predicted result? Take the time to decide which method of statistical analysis is most appropriate for this particular study.
- English and literally any topic: Write a paper about it!

Similarly, non-academic interests can be infused with education. Mathematical word problems can use names and situations from a student's favorite book or video game characters rather than generic placeholders. Art projects and essays can be assigned on essentially anything: paint your history chapter, write an essay about your favorite animal, write an essay about a historical painting you saw of your favorite animal! Think outside the box with topics rarely taught in schools today: fashion, engineering, philosophy, macroeconomics, comedy, entomology, dance, and endless other ideas. Spanish and French are great and all, but how could your student benefit from learning Mandarin, Sign Language, Swahili, Vietnamese, Braille? Think about the languages of your community: Vietnamese is the third most-spoken language in Texas and represents a major portion of the socioeconomic ecosystem of Dallas-Fort Worth; Minnesota has a thriving Somali refugee community in the twin cities of Minneapolis-St. Paul. Why not teach your child the language their ancestors spoke, whether that be Zulu, Welsh, Yiddish, Arabic, Urdu, or Old English? The possibilities are almost literally endless!

How can you encourage your student to turn their hobby into a passion, or even a career? John Cochran, *Survivor* super-fan and winner of *Survivor: Caramoan*, wrote an award-winning essay for Harvard Law about the show's jury system and its legal implications before going on to compete in it himself (and consequently winning a million dollars: an example of a particularly profitable hobby!). Most of the people creating the video games your kid loves started by playing them just as emphatically as your kid does, they just took the time to understand the mechanics on a deeper level…the same applies to the people who create films, paintings, books, and more.

Public schools offer Individualized Education Plans (IEPs) to accommodate different learners. Sometimes those needs are discovered, remedies are determined, and they are implemented quickly. However, just like the process of turning an aircraft carrier around, it can also take quite some time, and much like asking for permission to land on an aircraft carrier, they may not offer this to you if they don't feel you need it. Homeschooling removes all the hoop-jumping, the butt-kissing, the on-your-knees-pleading, the justifying, the testing, and the questions, ad nauseum. Everyone talks about these plans to fix public education: "if we could just get the funding," "if we just elected my preferred candidate," "if we just applied these research findings," etc. But changing and implementing new laws is a long and arduous process! Will we get recess back and new books next year? I don't know, but the homeschooler down the street saw an article online about the benefits of time spent outside and their kid was reading their history book in the backyard five minutes later. Will your school be forced to teach abstinence-only sex education to accommodate religious students? Will your school teach a detailed sex education curriculum you don't find appropriate? As a homeschooler you are free from the politics, logistics, and restrictions schools suffer from. The only exception: if you are the homeschooling coordinator of the home but not the breadwinner, you still might have to filibuster for funding.

Looking Back with Noel: My Encounter with Differentiation

I feel like "differentiation" has become the hottest new term in education recently, but we sometimes struggle to explain exactly what it is; in fact, I feel we struggle to imagine what it actually looks like when put into action. Personal experiences have done more for me in terms of understanding the realities of differentiation than all the papers I've ever read. For that reason, I want to share the story of my first encounter with differentiation with you.

When I was a kid, I attended a two-week-long summer math camp for advanced students at Texas A&M University. Many years later (but maybe not as many as you'd think), when I was a rising senior at A&M myself, I got the unique and surreal opportunity to return to this camp as a counselor rather than an attendee. My boss, Philip Yasskin, the same professor who taught me there when I was nine years old and who still ran the program, told me something that had an incredible impact on my understanding of student learning and differentiation.

If you've ever worked with gifted kids before, it should come as no shock to you that we were dealing with a lot of hyperactivity and intensity in this group. They were generally well-behaved, but some activities just got them so excited that we were basically herding cats. I stopped by one of the lab classes to see how everyone was doing and noticed that underneath the rows of computer desks, one kid was crawling around in the bevy of wires and legs. The other kids certainly seemed to notice him bumping around down there, but they didn't appear to really care. Meanwhile, the instructor was casually explaining circle homothety as if nothing was happening. I would've asked him to stop, but none of the other staff did, so I figured something else was going on. A few minutes later, I bumped into the math professor running the program and ask him what the deal is with that kid. "Yeah, that's just how he listens," he explained.

How he listens? That phrase confused me. If someone asked how one listens, what would you say? What does listening look like, and what is it for? I think at some point, we would all roughly describe listening as paying attention and not really doing anything else. If you're really listening, you won't play with your phone. If you're really paying attention, you'll look directly at the person speaking. You'll nod, "mm-hmm," and ask appropriate questions—all of which are considered "active listening skills." Just sitting quietly is considered "passive listening." Meanwhile, I'm wondering what kind of listening involves crawling around under tables.

"If you ask him about class afterward, it's clear he remembers everything," the professor continued.

"What about the other students? Doesn't it distract them?" I then asked (obviously).

"They can get over it. Eventually, they'll need to learn to pay attention in a non-ideal atmosphere: it comes in handy."

He said all of this like it was the most obvious, unquestionable thing: to me, it was like nonchalantly confirming the existence of unicorns; to him, it was like nonchalantly confirming the existence of horses.

So many things "clicked" for me after that conversation. How many times had I gone to the library and been unable to study because of someone else's phone conversation or the crunching of potato chips? Maybe if I had been exposed to more "background noise" or other natural distractors in study environments, I would've developed better coping mechanisms. I reflected on the innumerable times my mom would read to me when I was a kid while I drew, while I did handstands, while I worked on a sewing project, and how much easier it was for me to focus on the text than when I was reading to myself in my head. My mom even read to me while I was getting dental work done (yep, no excuses there either). Nothing gets you interested in hearing about World History quite like having someone operate on your mouth! To be fair, the dentist and staff loved it, so she could say she had a captive audience.

I didn't realize until that casual chat with the professor that I had been unconsciously accepting some of the arbitrary constraints of traditional education. Why do we all sit in the same chairs in rows of desks? Why do we all face the teacher in the front of the room? Why are doodling, moving, or even daydreaming considered punishable offenses in school? Even more importantly, why can't we have squishy chairs, beanbags, and loveseats? Why can't we sit in a circle, or in small groups for discussion? Couldn't we rethink the role of doodling, moving, and daydreaming?

I don't think the answer to any of these questions is "because research supports this as best practices." I can't prove it's random, but I can certainly say that my experience has led me to appreciate the value of flexibility. It also helped me to appreciate the diverse ways in which students can express their excitement and interest in a topic. I stopped seeing classroom management as "herding cats" and started seeing it as helping each student follow their own individual path to learning as best they can. I stopped seeing authority as a punishment/reward cycle and started seeing it as an opportunity to connect with students. I stopped seeing some kids as "problem students" and others as "well-behaved" and started seeing their needs in terms of wanting "more attention" or "more autonomy," respectively. I stopped focusing solely on what I needed to be teaching to students and started considering what I could be learning from them.

This might be a ridiculous comparison, but I think of the Jedi and Sith codes from the *Star Wars* universe. While many people think of Jedi as the "good guys" and the Sith as the "bad guys," it's always been a bit more complicated, especially in the extended universe. The Jedi believe that human emotion, even love, is a weakness and a distraction. The Sith see emotions as the only honest, truthful thing to be found in the universe, and try to harness it as a power instead of suppressing it. The Jedi/Sith dichotomy, at its core, does not represent good versus evil, but simply two conflicting extremes. The more recent films have focused more on the importance of balance, rather than one or the other. I think a lot of education has taken a Jedi approach to children: "There is no emotion, there is peace… there is no passion, there is serenity." This may be a decent approach if you're a monk learning how to lift rocks, perhaps not so good for a teacher. For all the talk of "developing student passion," educators often spend so much time doing whatever exactly prevents students from pursuing their passions. A student finishes his work early and begins reading a novel in the middle of the test room. He asks 25 questions in 25 minutes. He has trouble sitting down during his work and feels the need to stand up, do cartwheels, jog in a circle. He questions authority, he questions assignments, he questions everything.

He criticizes other students' work and has trouble taking no for an answer. He talks out of turn. He's high energy and low focus. He's exhibiting some of the most common behaviors of a highly creative and intelligent student. Would you call him "gifted"? Would you call him "creative"? Or would you call him a "problem student"? Everybody wants a young Picasso in their art class. But do you want him in your math class?

I don't think you need to defect to the Sith and start shooting lightning out of your hands. Encouraging creativity doesn't mean throwing all sense of stability out of the window. I'm just saying that there's a balance to be found when you start questioning what you thought you knew about best practices in education. "You must unlearn what you have learned," as Jedi Master Yoda says. Better yet, step away from what works best when you're trying to herd cats and work towards what works best when you're trying to create a diverse, passionate classroom. That is what I try to do.

Chapter 3
Developing Brains

The way your brain develops is an extraordinarily complex process and includes distinct phases at different points in your life. A toddler has more synapses, or connections, between brain cells than adults. As the brain matures, it prunes these connections. This pruning process is vital as it allows us to reinforce the connections that are essential to survival in society. By adolescence, the human brain is hard-wired for risk-taking. Evolution dictates that it is important for this risk-taking to take place. Young adults need to have the courage for and to see the value in expanding the gene pool by straying from traditional social norms to engage in what might be considered "risky" behavior. Exploration and the search to expand the gene-pool has proven a very necessary attribute to preserve human existence. Humans must seek mates outside of their immediate families and tribes to off-set the propagation of damaging rare mutations and recessive traits. So which parts of the human brain are we most interested in here?

The prefrontal cortex covers the front part of the frontal lobe. It is this area that allows us to engage in higher-order executive functions, such as decision-making, inhibition control, attention control, working memory, and personality expression. This is the area that resists peer-pressure and has the ability to anticipate future consequences, certainly a key issue when trying to understand the teen brain.

The limbic system is a network of nerves within the brain that controls our basic emotions and rudimentary functions, such as pleasure, sexual desire, and fear. It is the limbic system that also drives the desire for reward-seeking. Peer-approval is tremendously rewarding and drives the pleasure centers within the limbic system.

During adolescence, the brain is reshaped. Some neural connections are strengthened, while others are eliminated or pruned. Hormones, along with the myriad other stresses of adolescence, mean this reshaping can cause instability and frustration. Furthermore, the coping mechanisms that are developed during this period will ultimately inform the very person the teen becomes in the future. This is a time when the brain is vulnerable; incorrect or poorly adapted connections may be made and manifest in mental illness. Adults who struggle with addiction or other stress-related problems can often trace this back to teenage traumas and situations.

In a healthy, mature brain, the prefrontal cortex and the limbic system should be both well-developed and well-connected. The prefrontal cortex acts as a way of balancing the emotional, pleasure-seeking limbic system. In the teen brain, the prefrontal cortex remains underdeveloped while the limbic system is very active. Furthermore, the prefrontal cortex and its connection to the rest of the brain is slow due to nerve tracts that are not fully insulated with a coating of myelin. So, while a teenager may be able to articulate and understand that a behavior is risky or result in negative outcomes, the limbic system overrides the ability of the prefrontal cortex to inhibit that behavior in real-time, especially in the presence of peers. Teens are hard-wired to seek peer approval, and by doing so, the executive functioning mechanisms are neglected as their connections are slower.

How will this ultimately impact on the life of a young adult? Their limbic system is over-expressed, and inhibition underdeveloped and poorly connected to the rest of the brain; this means that teenagers are less likely to have the insight to know what's best for themselves. Decisions regarding drug use, sexual activity, dietary choices, and planning for the future are impaired in adolescence. However, this is also the time in life where parents often allow them more freedom and tend to be more hands-off. Further, amidst this profound brain remodeling and the pressures of transitioning from childhood to adulthood, they are thrust out of the safety of their homes, away from the loving and supervisorial eyes of their parents, and into the world or onto college campuses with many accompanying stressors. Unsurprisingly, they can be woefully ill-equipped to deal with this major life-change. In fact, only 54.8% of all students who begin study at any post-secondary institution will complete a degree within 6 years (Shapiro et al., 2016).

One advantage of early or local college is the pre-teen and teen will likely remain in their current stable life situation as they embark on a new educational journey. Parents can be more present and involved, helping guide their decision-making. Early identification of excess stress, poor coping mechanisms, anxiety, depression, or risky peer-influences can allow the student's support system to mitigate the negative outcomes on the adolescent brain. Ensuring adequate nutrition, sleep, counsel, and advocacy increase the likelihood of a successful college experience for a teenager. A young teen in college will surely benefit from this multi-pronged support and complete a degree plan with less stress than a young adult trying to transition into the world.

A teen who has completed a degree plan, and possibly even a graduate degree, prior to entering into the world as an adult, is no doubt better equipped to transition into adulthood. While uncertainty and apprehension naturally accompany any major life transition, creating your place in the world as a new adult can be a particular source of anxiety. Yet having your academic credentials and educational training complete offers young people the opportunity to explore at a much earlier stage in their lives. Having the option to do meaningful work while still nurturing the optimism and idealism of youth can be a source of great motivation for the young person, giving them a degree of freedom and flexibility to make adjustments without compromising their education. Specifically for a young woman, there are distinct advantages if she can complete her educational training before her mid-twenties and prior to the onset of other life events that may compromise her ability to fully engage in her career and educational developments.

Looking Back with Haley: Finding My Voice

When you are a child with big ideas, strong opinions, and lots to say, it can be crushing when the adults in your life fail to appreciate these attributes in you. So often, children are expected to be seen and not heard. Parents and teachers impose strict rules to maintain order. Adults tasked with caring for children are rarely well-respected for their skills. Even when it comes to medicine, the physicians that treat children are the lowest paid.

As a child raised in traditional classrooms, I was often hushed. I am a very auditory learner; I enjoy the interactive sharing of ideas and discussions that spring-board new solutions and solidify old lessons learned. Oftentimes in class while the teacher was lecturing, I would eagerly jump at the opportunity to engage in dialogue. I would raise my hand, but never wait to be called on. I would speak out of turn because what I had to say was only relevant to the point being discussed at that particular moment; I didn't want to allow the conversation to move forward until my question had been answered. Most of the time, I was the only one in class that seemed to care about what was being taught, so I didn't feel like I was interrupting anyone's education. However, the teacher had a lesson plan she had to get through by the end of the term, so she never had time to engage in tangents or discussions. I was forced to sit still, take notes, say nothing, and learn the lesson in the singular way it was presented.

The more this became the norm, the more I started to dislike school. I associated learning new things with school, so by association, as my distaste for school grew, I also started to dislike learning.

Social time at school was very regimented in an effort to avoid bullying and bad behavior, and it was hardly representative of true socialization (which itself may include bullying and bad behavior at times that cannot be avoided). Thus, oftentimes my voice went unheard or unappreciated. My ideas were only expressed in the hurried after-school car-ride, or to distracted parents at the end of the work/school day.

Learning was painful. Socializing was impossible. Everything about school was torturous…and homeschooling made all that pain disappear.

When I started homeschooling, my mother made a conscious decision to find creative outlets for my self-expression. I started engaging in speech and debate. I participated in a competition with Jack and Jill of America. I joined spoken word groups like Big Thought and Journeyman Ink. And I started writing and performing Spoken Word at Daverse Lounge.

Spoken Word is a form of poetry that is performed live. It involves all the challenge and creativity of writing a poem combined with the added anxiety of public speaking. When I went to Daverse Lounge and performed for the first time, I was petrified. Since I had written the piece, I was worried not only about performing my poem, but how people would react to the content. Spoken word poems are often deeply personal and often address controversial or sensitive topics. Once I started reciting the poem (which I had diligently practiced to the point of perfect memorization) I gained confidence. Halfway through the poem, I realized that I had captured the attention of over 500 people, and everyone was absorbing and receiving my words. In that moment came the realization: "my voice has power." I felt appreciated and empowered.

Over the past few years since then, I have performed with my sister and on my own numerous times, and each time I have been blown away by the acceptance and open-mindedness of the Spoken Word community. I met so many amazing people that first night, and during my time in the community, my relationships have grown. There are buses of students from nearby schools that bring their own poems, so I am able to meet and listen to local like-minded peers who have incredible perspectives and poetry to share.

I have been asked about socialization and life outside homeschooling many times, and specifically about how I was able to "find myself" without traditional schooling. "Finding myself" has been much more straight-forward for me in many ways since leaving public school, rather than more difficult. School was, the vast majority of my life, an institution that only served to silence me into compliance, where the blind acceptance of a biased rhetoric under the veil of "essential academic skills" is not only expectation but commandment. The only reason I am able to interact in an appropriate and authentic way is that I was allowed to express myself openly as a homeschooled student and then allowed to enter college early. Instead of plowing energy into trying to be like everybody else, I had the time and encouragement to engage in introspective, diverse, dynamic communities of artists and activists that encouraged me to find my own voice!

In a world that celebrates conformity, I am proud to be atypical. I was born to a Black mom and a White dad. I am a homeschooled high school graduate. I am a Black girl math whiz. I play the harp in the Fort Worth Youth Orchestra on Sundays, and on Mondays, I don my sabre fencing attire and pick up a sword to dominate the strip. On every level, I defy expectations and stereotypes. I am atypical. I defy old (negative) stereotypes and create new (positive) ones.

Looking Back with Myiesha: A Different Type of Kid

Haley was a ten-year-old in fifth grade. With an August birthday, she was almost a full chronological year younger than the rest of her class. On top of this, there were many students who had been held back in a practice called "redshirting" (where parents intentionally keep their kids in pre-school to allow for an extra year of development). This made Haley a full two years younger than many of the other students—including her best friend.

Dad stayed home with Haley for the first year of her life, and thereafter she was in institutional day-care or traditional school continuously. I had heard (and now believe) that the time to really pay extra attention to your child is as they approach adolescence. At this age, small alterations and slightly refocused efforts can have a huge pay-off. However, neglecting to be an active and present parent at this stage can prove quite detrimental. I often tell parents that many people can take excellent care of your infant or toddler. They only require loving hands and patience. Contrariwise, only a very select few people can offer the mothering or fathering required by a tween or teenager.

We knew Haley was going to expand our parenting skills. She was born independent and has proven, time and time again, that she requires parents that have the energy and wherewithal to be innovative and involved. She was an early talker, outgoing and social. She was strong-willed and opinionated from the day she was born. She mastered every developmental milestone months earlier than expected. We knew Haley was a different kind of child when she rolled across the room at eight weeks old to "investigate" a newspaper with her mouth!

Haley had some minor issues with friend relationships, listening, maturity, and self-control. She was one of only two children of color in her class, and one of ten in her grade-level (who numbered over 500) and she was often misunderstood and left confused. Growing up is complicated and school seemed to be complicating it further for Haley. She found it difficult to wind down unless downtime was incorporated into her routine. Since traditional school has students on-the-go all day, she simply wasn't able to be the best version of herself.

As a strong-willed girl, Haley often volunteered for leadership positions and stepped into those roles with a level of authority that was off-putting to many of her peers. As the "teacher's pet," she was not invited to classmate's birthday parties, and she was left to cycle through friend groups oftentimes on the fringe, and only for as long as she was willing to share her answers or help with coursework. One month she may have a friend in the math club, the next month she's trying to dye her hair blond so she can be popular.

Obviously, school should never be expected to teach your child everything they need to know in order to live a great life. Therefore, it is necessary to fill in these educational gaps. To do this I implemented a supplemental curriculum which was designed to enhance her classroom academic lessons. However, after waking up early and spending a long day at school, there was little energy at the end of the day to engage in any meaningful academic enrichment. It was then that I realized that the current way we educate our students was just not going to work for Haley. She was not learning about life and about the world in a way that would be applicable to her.

Nonetheless, I had quite a bit of anxiety about my decision to homeschool her, and then accelerate her. I tried to remind myself that this entire thing was not about me; it was about Haley. Her triumphs, and her tribulations, are hers to celebrate, enjoy, and learn from. No self-respecting mother would proclaim otherwise!

But it was my decision to graduate her from high school at 13. She blindly and wholeheartedly trusted my judgement. However, the confidence she had in my advice and actions on her behalf was, oftentimes, much higher than the confidence I had in myself. I grappled with this, and two recurrent themes arose in my own mind: First, however awesome she is at fourteen, she'll be even *more* awesome at eighteen, no doubt. Even if she seems to be a perfect college candidate at this age, another four years couldn't do anything but make her better. Having her start early makes her less competitive for graduate programs since her marks won't be as high, nor her accomplishments as great, as the 22-year-old version of herself (the time/age at which she'd be applying on a traditional path). Second, would she be mad at me for missing high school? Especially if she doesn't do as well on this path as is necessary to go directly into the next phase of her life?

In a nutshell, I had the traditional path to an Ivy league school in mind. This path included AP exams, CLEP exams, dual enrollment courses, combined with science competition awards (Intel, Olympiads, Siemens) with a healthy dose of original research added to the mix. All while playing first chair harp (exotic, right?) on the Community Youth Orchestra, *and* becoming a fencing champion (or at least nationally ranked). If she was feeling very studious, I had a progressive plan to study for SAT/ACT exam and in the process also get in those 3 SAT subject exams.

Sure, it wouldn't be the end of the world if she couldn't accomplish all of these things. But if she was to be on task, this plan starts in eighth grade! Otherwise, really, there's no good way to work it all in.

The best laid plans often go awry.

Some people are placed on Earth to make huge shifts. I'm certainly biased as her parent, but I believe Haley to be one of them. Traditional school (that box of conformity and limitations) is not often conducive to realizing the full potential of these people. People like Haley are unmotivated by external accolades (such as grades and scores) and only pretend to care because they care about the opinion of the people who actually care. The people who do care are very important, and worth the effort of trying to go against the grain and fit into the box. But, Haley really did not enjoy being inside that box.

I also knew that the box was a necessary step—both for practical reasons (you need to learn some things) and also for more superficial reasons (people accept you, which has a legitimizing factor for any person, but especially a woman of color). So my goal became getting Haley into and out of that box as soon as she was ready. Otherwise, I feared, she would either lose part of herself in the box, or (just as detrimental) never complete the box stage of her life and miss opportunities to influence the world...and we couldn't have that.

She actually said to me: "I don't want everything to be about college. I get it's important, but it's going to take too long to do what you're asking me to do."

What I *heard* was: I am not motivated to work hard to get into a good/prestigious college only to work harder to graduate from that school and go to medical school. I am not going to stay in school for twelve more years!

That day, I changed my plan. I went from "homeschool to Ivy to graduate school" to "let's get this crap done ASAP and we can figure the rest out later." The way I saw it, I had a thirteen-year-old daughter that listens to me, values me, and over whom I still have some influence. And the exams (TSI, CLEPS, IQ) demonstrate that she is capable and academically ready, today. She cares, today. She's home, today. And instead of languishing (amongst bad influences and hormonal teenagers at the local high school) why not just get started on that path, today?

Chapter 4
Stress and Executive Functioning

"Certainly, the game is rigged. Don't let that stop you. If you don't bet; you can't win."
Robert A. Heinlein, *Time Enough for Love (1973)*

In order to make the transition from being a dependent child to a productive adult, well-developed executive functioning skills are imperative. These skills include the ability to pay attention, to organize and plan, to remember and recall important information, to develop problem-solving skills through creative thinking, and to master self-control. As adolescents are entering high school and thinking about college, their brains are undergoing major re-wiring, including the hard-wired desire to engage in more risky behavior. Despite the fear this brings to parents, this is actually evolutionarily advantageous as it allows for human tribes to expand their gene-pool by seeking new and unfamiliar experiences without fear.

During this delicate time of transition where their frontal lobe is overshadowed by the limbic system, it is critically important to help adolescents gain some insight and develop skills that enhance executive functioning (EF). Traditional schools often fail to create an environment that fosters the development of those EF skills. Of particular concern is the fact that arbitrary and excessive amounts of stress will actually interfere with the development and expression of these requisite executive functioning skills which can have life-long adverse effects on their development.

How does stress affect our brains?

Multiple studies have demonstrated that psychological stress can actually cause changes in DNA. DNA, or deoxyribonucleic acid, are biomolecules that provide the instructions that our cells need to divide, develop, and grow. DNA tells our cells what their jobs are and how and when to do them. For example, when cells divide, it is under the direction of their DNA. Therefore, healthy DNA is critical to physical and mental health. Not only does stress adversely affect how the genes on the DNA are expressed, it actually causes physical changes to the DNA that could contribute to neuropsychiatric disorders and shortened life expectancy.

Telomeres are found on the very ends of our DNA molecules. They are the protective casing that encapsulates our DNA (like the sheath on the end of your shoelace which prevents it from unraveling). The length of a telomere is an indicator of aging—shorter telomeres reflect a more advanced age. During DNA replication (which is necessary and happens in every cell division in our bodies throughout our lifetime), the telomere is ever so slightly shortened. Over the course of a lifetime, there are a set number of times a cell can replicate and once no further replication can take place, it dies. When enough of these cells reach the point of "telomere depletion," the entire organism dies. We die. Thus, telomeres are critical to the longevity of life.

Stress causes a shortening of telomeres. There are groups of humans that experience stress differently and can have stress-related accelerated biological telomere shortening from the mainstream population—such as differences in background or skin color. Further, it has been demonstrated that adversity in childhood has a negative impact on telomere length. Therefore, children that do not "fit in" to "normal" school situations may suffer worse health outcomes and decreased life expectancy due to the chronic stressful situations that they endure.

Executive functioning relies mainly on the prefrontal cortex and interconnected neural regions. When a person is sad, angry, lonely, or otherwise emotionally or physically stressed, their ability to solve problems and exercise caution diminishes. Depending on genetic make-up and hereditary predispositions, this compromise in executive functional ability as a result of stress can be devastating. Stress is generally thought to impair executive functioning and may manifest as an apparent learning disability or psychiatric illness in otherwise healthy people.

Where does stress come from?

We've all heard of stress. According to Merriam-Webster, stress is "a state of mental or emotional strain or tension resulting from adverse or very demanding circumstances." Some stress is beneficial, motivating, and necessary. Feelings of worry and anxiety encourage better preparation for difficult situations. Fear and apprehension may offer protection by guiding us away from unsafe environments. The fight or flight stress response actually enhances short-term performance and cognition. Indeed, stress is a necessary part of life, and in appropriate doses is beneficial.

However, repeated or ongoing stress is counter-productive and damaging. Not only does stress affect our very DNA, as discussed, but it causes inflammation in the body which contributes to the development of diseases such as metabolic syndrome (which include obesity, diabetes, and hypertension), as well as having autoimmune, cardiac, and neurological manifestations. Unfortunately, typical school children are subjected to this chronic, unhealthy, damaging form of ongoing stress from very early ages and sadly, as a result, society has seen a spike in associated physical and mental illnesses.

Traditional school systems are high-stakes, high-pressure environments. Mandated state testing and college-entry examinations are often preceded by years of skill-and-drill preparation with parents often paying excessive, out-of-pocket sums for private tutoring and prep-classes in an attempt to maximize scores.

The school schedule is itself one that is based on societal logistics whereby parents typically have to be at work by 9 a.m., therefore school has to start at 8 a.m. or earlier to accommodate the adults. This schedule leaves children and teens in a constant state of sleep-deprivation which is further associated with adverse physical and psychological manifestations that affect behavior, learning, and relationships. Most older children would be better served by later start times, more sleep, healthier food options, and later bedtimes. However, the traditional schooling system is unable or unwilling to incorporate these necessary elements, despite what can only be described as begging by the American Academy of Pediatrics and the Center for Disease Control.

Finally, parental anxiety is prevalent as life becomes an endless, terrible competition. The only path to success- both for parent and for child- is to win a coveted university spot at a top tier school. This is well exemplified by the Operation: Varsity Blues scandal where dozens of students with high-profile and/or wealthy parents were gaining acceptance into top colleges and universities via bribery and cheating on entrance exams. The validation that our society bestows upon students, and their parents, when they play by the arbitrary rules of this crazy game pushes them beyond healthy limits. It is a game that requires myriad superlatives ranging from outstanding GPA and test scores, to impressive and meaningful extracurriculars, community service commitments, and profound personal statements; and this all begins in primary school. Students realize that their performance affects their parents' sense of worth and achievement, which then leads to greater amounts of stress on the student to please their parents. Predictably, this adds to the cycle of performance anxiety and chronic stress.

Nurturing the Development of Executive Functioning

Brené Brown's 2015 book, *Daring Greatly*, speaks eloquently about her research on vulnerability; she articulates the fear that we have some guilty secret shortcoming which if other people knew, would make them push you away. It is a sense of unworthiness. Yet for connection to happen, we must allow ourselves to be really, truly seen. Her research showed that the only variable between those with a strong sense of love and belonging and those who don't, was a personal conviction of being worthy of love and belonging. People who feel they are in a loving, nurturing relationship have the courage to be imperfect.

Who better to offer a loving, nurturing relationship, than parents? Parents want to encourage, support, and push a bit when needed; they want their kids to be their best version of who they can be. Yet, there is a big difference between the excitement and exhilaration of being challenged versus the anxiety of being stressed. That difference isn't always an easy thing for a parent to see or for a kid to articulate. Yes, it is an extraordinary challenge to find that balance, but it's also an important one.

Inhibitory Control

Inhibitory control is the proverbial secret sauce of executive functioning. It helps children to be less impulsive, be more persistent, and better able to regulate attention. In an amazing longitudinal study over more than 32 years, researchers showed that children with better inhibitory control would, as adults, some 30 years later, have better health, higher income, and better jobs, fewer run-ins with the law, and—big shock—were happier. So how do we learn inhibitory control? Through better executive function skills. And what is the main obstacle we have in honing those skills? Stress. Yep, what hurts our kids is being stressed, sad, lonely or physically inactive. Not a shocking revelation. So other than trying to avoid those negatives, what else can help with inhibitory control? Mindful movement practices like Tai Chi. Yoga can be good too, though competitivity and embarrassment can sometimes diminish its effectiveness. Overall, kids who are more physically active and have better aerobic fitness also have better executive functioning skills.

What should come as no surprise is that what truly matters most in early childhood education is not the number of children, nor the caregiver-to-child ratio, nor even having the best materials, but the caring relationship between the adult and the children. A caring teacher can make all the difference, and sadly, the converse is true; a bad teacher can traumatize a child.

Incidentally, the same principle is true in psychotherapy. What's most important is *not* the type of therapy practiced: the most successful clinical outcomes were achieved by those who care deeply about their patients and were able to communicate that caring to their patients.

The good news is that maternal sensitivity and warmth can completely override the effects of early adversity on telomere length. There is insufficient research on fathers to say whether this is also true of a paternal link, but it is certainly inferred. Responsive parenting from a caring, warm adult is the single greatest mitigating factor to early adversity of trauma. Responsive parenting entails listening and taking turns in conversation with your child. It also aids language development, literacy, and maturation of brain regions critical for language. The conversation that takes place in the context of reading seems to have more benefit than the reading itself. The critical variable is the number of conversational turns taken, namely, talking *with* the child, listening and responding, and not merely talking to or at the child.

The concept of mind-body connection has been well-documented in scientific research. The cognitive, spiritual, social, emotional, and physical health of a person are intertwined. Focusing exclusively on academic instruction and standardized testing, as public education tends to do, is not the most effective or efficient way to improve cognition, as it tends to ignore the other parts of the mind-body paradigm.

The fear of making a mistake is a huge source of anxiety. The fear you will appear unsuccessful is another source of mental anguish. Carol Dweck famously pioneered understanding of the growth mindset, which argued that errors and failed attempts must be treated as learning opportunities, as an opportunity for improvement. Young people need activities that touch their hearts and minds, inspiring them, challenging them to reach high, building their self-confidence and pride. And they need that without the heavy toll of excess stress. One of the innumerable benefits of homeschooling is that there is more time for that caring relationship to be maintained. Finding ways in your family, both big and small, to minimize unhealthy stress and nurture executive functioning skills is a noble and necessary goal for the health and happiness of everyone.

References

Adolescent Sleep Working Group, Committee on Adolescence, & Council on School Health. (2014). School start times for adolescents. *Pediatrics, 134*(3), 642-649. https://doi.org/10.1542/peds.2014-1697

Allan, J. L., McMinn, D., & Daly, M. (2016). A bidirectional relationship between executive function and health behavior: Evidence, implications, and future directions. *Frontiers in Neuroscience, 10*(386). https://doi.org/10.3389/fnins.2016.00386

Arnsten, A. F. T. (2009). Stress signaling pathways that impair prefrontal cortex structure and function. *Nature Reviews Neuroscience, 10*, 410-422. https://doi.org/10.1038/nrn2648

Asok, A., Bernard, K., Roth, T. L., Rosen, J. B., & Dozier, M. (2013). Parental responsiveness moderates the association between early-life stress and reduced telomere length. *Developmental Psychopathology, 25*(3), 577-585. https://doi.org/10.1017/S0954579413000011

Beiter, R., Nash, R., McCrady, M., Rhoades, D., Linscomb, M., Clarahan, M., Sammut, S. (2015). The prevalence and correlates of depression, anxiety, and stress in a sample of college students. *Journal of Affective Disorders,* 17390–17396.

Berman, A. L. (2009). Depression and suicide. In Gotlib, I. H., Hammen, C. L. (Eds.), *Handbook of depression* (2nd ed., pp. 510–530). New York, NY: Guilford.

Blackburn, E. & Epel, E. (2017). *The telomere effect.* Grand Central Publishing.

Brown, B. (2015). *Daring greatly: How the courage to be vulnerable transforms the way we live, love, parent, and lead.* Penguin.

Castelli, D. M., Hillman, C. H., Buck, S. M., Erwin, H. E. (2007). Physical fitness and academic achievement in third- and fifth-grade students. *Journal of Sport and Exercise Psychology, 29*(2), 239-252. https://doi.org/10.1123/jsep.29.2.239

Coimbra, B. M., Carvalho, C. M., Moretti, P. N., Mello, M. F., & Belangero, S. I. (2017). Stress-related telomere length in children: A systematic review. *Journal of Psychiatric Research, 3*(23), 47-54. https://doi.org/10.1016/j.jpsychires.2017.03.023

Dweck, C. (2008). *Mindset: The new psychology of success.* Random House Digital.

Geronimus, A. T., Hicken, M. T., Pearson, J. A., Seashols, S. J., Brown, K. L. & Dawson Cruz, T. (2010). Do US Black women experience stress-related accelerated biological aging? A novel theory of Black-White differences in telomere length. *Human Nature, 21*(1), 19-38. https://doi.org/10.1007/s12110-010-9078-0

Melhuish, E. C., Lloyd, E., Martin, S., & Mooney, A. (1990). Type of childcare at 18 months- II. Relations with cognitive and language development. *The Journal of Child Psychology and Psychiatry, 31*(6), 861-870.

Moffitt, T. E., Arseneault, L., Belsky, D., Dickson, N., Hancox, R. J., Harrington, HL., Houts, R., Poulton, R., Roberts, B. W., Ross, S., Sears, M. R., Thomson, W. M., & Caspi, A. (2011). A gradient of childhood self-control predicts health, wealth, and public safety. *Proceedings of the National Academy of Sciences of the United States of America, 108*(7), 2693-2698. https://doi.org/10.1073/pnas.1010076108

Rewak, M., Buka, S., Prescott, J., De Vivo, I., Luocks, E. B., Kawachi, I., Non, A. L., & Kubzansky, L. D. (2014). Race-related health disparities and biological aging: Does rate of telomere shortening differ across Blacks and Whites? *Biological Psychology, 99*, 92-99. https://doi.org/10.1016/j.biopsycho.2014.03.007

Scudder, M. R., Federmeier, K. D., Raine, L. B., Direito, A., Boyd, J. K., & Hillman, C. H. (2014). The association between aerobic fitness and language processing in children: Implications for academic achievement. *Brain and Cognition,* 87, 140-152. https://doi.org/10.1016/j.bandc.2014.03.016

Shields, G. S., Sazma, M. A., Yonelinas, A. P. (2016). The effects of acute stress on core executive functions: A meta-analysis and comparison with cortisol. *Neuroscience and Biobehavioral Reviews, 68*, 651-668. https://doi.org/10.1016/j.neubiorev.2016.06.038

Twenge, J. M., Joiner, T. E., Rogers, M. L., & Martin, G. N. (2018). Increases in depressive symptoms, suicide-related outcomes, and suicide rates among U.S. adolescents after 2010 and links to increased new media screen time. *Clinical Psychological Science, 6*(1), 3–17. https://doi.org/10.1177/2167702617723376

Wampold, B. (2001). *The great psychotherapy debate: Methods, models, and conclusions.* L. Erlbaum.

Yao, B., Cheng, Y., Wang, Z., Li, Y., Chen, L., Huang, L., Chang, W., Chen, D., Wu, H., Tang, B., & Jin, P. (2017). DNA N6-methyladenine is dynamically regulated in the mouse brain following environmental stress. *Nature Communications, 8.* https://doi.org/10.1038/s41467-017-01195-y

Looking Back with Noel: My First "F"

We all know natural talent is great, but hard work wins out in the end. For most of my education, I had done pretty well without ever having to try *that* hard. This is not good for the development of executive functioning skills, essentially because students get used to relying on talent rather than work ethic. Once they hit their first challenge, they don't know how to handle it academically or psychologically and it can have a devastating impact on their psyche. In avoidance of this, my mom (and homeschool principal) had put quite some effort into pushing me out of my intellectual comfort zone, and I was generally pretty good at handling the occasional underwhelming performance. Yet, I still somehow developed a bad habit of laziness. That problem reached its peak in my brief-and-mild-but-still-annoying "rebellious teenager" phase.

At community college, I had spent a decent portion of my time in class with earbuds in, listening to music, completely detached from what was actually going on. I also played a lot of solitaire on my laptop (yeah, I know, it was really bad). I focused enough of the time that I was able to maintain honors-level grades, but when I transferred to A&M, that delicate balance was finally thrown off. I had a Federal Government class that was not only completely uninteresting to me, but also quite difficult. Our professor was very smart and resourceful, but still a bit unpredictable and a ruthless grader. This is the kind of guy who is important enough to write his own textbook and then, when the Pearson representative comes in to talk about all the resources available on the Pearson webpage, he tears her to shreds and says the resources are stupid. I watched a Pearson representative named Katie fight back tears on one of our first days. But he could also pull magic tricks from time to time, so I thought he was alright, just intense.

I didn't pay any attention or study at all for our first test. Not sure what my plan was there; I got an F. I had never gotten a grade that low before and it was not an enjoyable feeling! I knew I deserved it, but my mom, not realizing that my studying was, in fact, non-existent, insisted I talk to him during his office hours about what I could do to improve my grade.

I remember having a sense of blind optimism as I walked into his office, but even from the beginning, I think he was somewhat incredulous as to why I was even speaking with him...perhaps he saw me as a lost cause already at this point. What kind of student doesn't care enough to completely avoid studying and fail the test miserably, but cares enough to come to your office to discuss it afterwards?

There was an air of disgust to his attitude, perhaps some morbid amusement as well. Most noticeable I think was his confusion, because he didn't seem to understand what I hoped to gain from meeting with him since I (in his mind, not that he wasn't right) had no interest in his subject. To his credit, he did help me work my way through the correct answers, but he also felt the need to tell me that I had selected not just the wrong answers, but the "most wrong" answers.

"See, this question here, you selected 'tax reform,' that's so irrelevant you might as well have put 'blue cows'!"

That's not fair, dude, tax reform sounds like government stuff!

Realizing how difficult it would be to even get a B at this point, I opted to drop the class. In Texas, you can only drop a limited number of classes in your undergraduate college career, so it made it feel like a big deal. I had already dropped one for scheduling issues at community college, and this was my second. By the end of my A&M career, I had racked up three. It had basically no impact on my ability to graduate according to my preferred timeline, and I was able to learn from the mistake without beating myself up too hard. Nonetheless, it was not a fun experience.

What's the takeaway here? Get comfortable with challenging material before going to college. Learn study skills and, above all, paying-attention skills. Don't hate yourself for making mistakes, but, you know, maybe avoid making them when you can. The great thing about early college is you get the chance to make these kinds of mistakes without worrying you're ruining your only shot at college. A perfect education isn't one that will prepare you for college so well that you will never mess up, just as perfect parenting isn't preventing stress from ever touching the life of your child. Education and parenting are both about preparing for mistakes, rather than working so hard that they'll never happen (even if that was possible). My hope is that this story leaves you feeling it's okay to make mistakes; you'll just have to handle the consequences with the greatest degree of maturity possible. But also, maybe the most obvious takeaway is to take out your earbuds and actually listen in class.

Looking Back with Nancy: When to Help and When Not to Help? That is the question.

Parenting kids has got to be the most subjective thing in the world: when to coddle, when to correct, when to criticize, when to keep your cool, and everything in between. When Noel was born, I had to have a scheduled C-section: she was born two-and-a-half weeks early. Having gone through parenting classes and read a reasonable amount of parenting books, I was determined to breastfeed my baby. However, it did not come as naturally as I was assured it would be by my Mom, a mother of five. "It's just like shellin' peas!" Having not been raised as a sharecropper's daughter, I had only shelled a limited amount of peas! We went through all five lactation consultants on staff at the hospital. She only nursed the first time, maybe an hour old, then never again. It was exhausting to pump and then still need to feed her. It was not helping my confidence as a new mom that I couldn't do what I was determined to do and what my body was designed for. We eventually paid for a lactation consultant to come to our house. She stripped Noel and weighed her on a digital scale. I showed her the chart of

Noel's feedings and how much I was pumping: we even went so far as to finger-feed Noel, as I was determined to breastfeed and did not want her to become accustomed to a bottle. This wise, seasoned, and gentle nurse was calming and reassuring. As a newborn, Noel was eating about 2-3 oz per feeding. She gently assured me that a baby wants to nurse, it indeed can be "like shellin' peas", with a little help now and again. After mere moments of coaching from her, Noel and I had it all figured out. She weighed her again on the digital scale. She had gained over 7 oz!

This lactation consultant was our new hero and I felt like a rock star! We peppered her with questions, and she answered them calmly and assuredly. She then said these magic words, "Soon enough, you will know this baby better than anyone else." That was hard to imagine. I wasn't nearly as confident in myself as she seemed to be. I wanted to believe my new hero, but it was almost inconceivable. My mom had basically said the same thing, but I didn't buy that either. My mom's analogy was that it didn't take long for me to understand the different meanings of my dog's barks, and thus it wouldn't take long to get my head around my newborn's cries and emotions too. I soon realized they were indeed both right. But dang, that in between time of not believing my wise mother and this paid professional, was straight up hard.

Fast forward to your kid. When do you offer a helping hand, so they don't flop so hard it crushes their soul? When do you let them fly, knowing full well they might simply fall? That is where the subjective decision-making comes into play. You think of your neighbor's son, who was coddled too much and now sleeps in the basement and can't hold a job. Or of your aunt who was so demanding and strict that her kid left for college, dropped out—never to come home again. Or maybe you know an amazing family with successful and happy kids. Or maybe you know all of the above and in between and how the circumstances are always unique and complex—just as people tend to be. Throw in the personalities of parents, siblings, shifts in culture and technology…it's a lot to navigate.

How I chose to help and not help Noel as she navigated unique waters as an early college student was indeed subjective; it might have been different had she been at public school, it might not. My style and choices are based on my personality, my parenting research, and the best I could do any given day. Without question, some days I was that rock star, and every now and again, I was awful. I was a fan of "love and logic" parenting and read Dr. Sears' books more than once. I totally identified with attachment-style parenting. I had read several other parenting books too, but Dr. Sears' body of work felt both intuitive and logical.

When should you bring your kid the lunch they forgot on the table and when should you let them go hungry (and learn from their mistakes)? It's a subjective decision. Will they have to take a big test with their stomach growling? Will they be light-headed for PE? Did they clearly understand the consequences of their decisions? Could they just use a little grace this time? There are a thousand other variables.

Teaching empathy, compassion, and kindness is best done by modeling those traits. Totalitarianism doesn't work nearly as well. You certainly don't want to raise your kid thinking that anything goes, and conversely, you don't want them to ever question that they are loved unconditionally. I benefited greatly from the wisdom of other moms. I also understood children so much better when reading about their development from parenting books. And I learned most from paying attention to and interacting with Noel and understanding her strengths and weaknesses.

Whether you are a fan of tough love or a hippie at heart, you have to make your own choices along the way. It's a big scary world out there some days and yet it is an amazing source of beauty and wonder too. You know your kiddo better than anyone else. Good luck.

Part 2
WHAT TO DO ABOUT IT

While traditional public and private schools may work relatively well for a portion of the population, there are large numbers of outliers that cannot be accommodated in our current system. One size never fits all, and it is very common that intellectually gifted children, children of color, English language learners, and children with learning differences are actively harmed by our attempts to force conformity using a system ill-equipped to meet their needs. For these reasons and countless others, homeschooling can be the preferable choice.

The opportunity to tailor your education is one of the most important aspects of homeschooling. Students have more control over what they learn and how they learn it. They can also go at their own pace without having to be bored or grow impatient while waiting for others to catch up. Conversely, if the student already understands the material or is picking the material up quickly they can move on to a higher level and work at their own pace without being held back. This choice helps maintain the mental well-being of the students. The flexibility, individuality, and the tailored environment of homeschooling help many students to thrive.

Homeschooling does, however, require a shift in mindset. A homeschooling parent accepts it as their parental responsibility to see that their child is educated. As such, they make it their priority to acquire and invite into the lives of their children the tools and strategies necessary for them to be successful. Their definition of success focuses on the needs of the child, and not what traditional school or society claims is "success." Homeschooling allows a parent to more holistically develop their child with a customized educational experience that promotes mental, emotional, spiritual, and physical health while affirming their child and their added value in our world.

References

Davidson Institute. (2020). *The Fallacy of a "One Size Fits All" Education.* [online] Available at: http://www.davidsongifted.org/Search-Database/entry/A10507 [Accessed 29 Jan. 2020].

Taylor, M. & Taylor Schlitz, H. (2019) *The Homeschool Alternative.* Taylored Publishing.

Chapter 5
Educating Our Children

It is certainly the easiest path to plop our kids in the school they are zoned for and leave it to the professionals to educate our children. For those fortunate few, the easiest option turns out to be the best. For most, though, it is more complex.

Like most everything in life, reasonable people can see things differently. This is certainly true of educational theories and trends. Some ideas sound good on paper but do not manifest well in practice. Sometimes, the latest and greatest plan seems like a positive step forward, yet it will disregard the tried and true methods that continue to work. Just as no one wants to have heart surgery "the same way my good ol' grandpappy had it," we usually prefer the latest technology and techniques available. However, there is always the fear that the most recent discoveries are still not thoroughly researched, and will later be seen as fads rather than frontiers. How do we know when the latest and greatest in educational policy is indeed such, or when we are discarding the tried and true? When is the collateral damage evaluated? To quote the Canadian rock band Rush in their song *Bravado* "We will pay the price, but we will not count the cost."

Above all, we must remember that different things work for different people. Howard Wainer's book, *Uneducated Guesses*, enumerates many instances of ideas put into practice under the guise of good policy when the statistics do not back them up. No Child Left Behind had bipartisan support in Congress but was not effective. Common Core was sold as a way to help American children compete globally, and almost 10 years later the results are entirely unimpressive. Sadly, it isn't as simple as bringing in new legislation or implementing the best policies from other countries and getting superior results. To discuss this in any detail would take several books to explain, and not be without a degree of controversy. So, let us instead focus here on our goal.

Our purpose is to provide knowledge, in the form or research, opinion, and our own anecdotal experiences—after all, knowledge is power. You may not yet have the power to change your circumstances as much as you like, but knowledge remains an extraordinary tool. We've highlighted the shortcomings of public education. Conversely, we are not implying that private and charter schools have a monopoly on sunshine and rainbows either. Not even the completely customizable homeschooling option is the be-all-and-end-all for everyone. Our goal is to give you power through knowledge to make more informed decisions for your family. As parents, we want to raise our children to be, at the very least, independent, moral, productive, happy, healthy, mature individuals who can take those skills and values into adulthood. If there were one perfect way to do that that worked for everyone, that absolutely that would be the way we would do it. Alas, no.

Technology is changing the landscape of our world so rapidly that what and how one might learn in school could easily become outdated in the near future. Thus, the best education should aim to ingrain a love of learning along with the knowledge of how to learn. The age of the Internet and access to information is a paradigm shift for us all. The ability to obtain a veritable treasure trove of data on any topic from the comfort of your couch and at the tap of your fingertips is nothing less than mind-boggling. To think we put a man on the moon with technology less powerful than the smartphones sitting in the palm of our hands is stupefying. The need to know how to extract information from this monumental influx of data and then process that into knowledge, and not just for a quiz, but to grasp and comprehend material is a critical skillset. To further complicate this situation, there is a need to interpret what data is fact, opinion, biased, agenda-driven, etc. Critical thinking skills come, not from rote memorization, but from applying information using changing parameters. Discernment comes from wisdom. Wisdom comes from experience. Experience comes over time when we are open to new approaches. Our current educational paradigm does not tend to celebrate this.

We might question the weighting of the contemporary school syllabus. For example, we often casually mention "the classics," but how much time does your child spend reading Shakespeare and The Federalist Papers? Furthermore, who defines what is a classic worth studying? The scope, perspective, and ranges of time taught through history are also changing. We still typically spend one year learning American history, as we have done for decades, yet as time moves forward, more history is created (obviously). What gets squeezed out? What is allowed and what is glossed over, if not completely ignored? Certainly, it has been documented that history is often sanitized, and the accomplishments of women and minorities diminished and/or relegated to only one month of study. In the same vein, is it truly critical to memorize math facts and formulae when we have calculators and powerful programs at our fingertips? So, should our kids learn more real-world skill sets while in the K-12 years? These are all fair questions and debatable topics, with divisive, ambiguous, or currently unknowable answers.

Imagine the level of bureaucracy standing between your child and learning. Federal, state, county, school district, school board, principal, teaching clusters, and teacher. One could argue if the learning is getting that much attention, it must produce an amazing product. Once again, as we shall see (and have seen), the statistics do not support this. Too many cooks spoil the pot, as it were.

College-readiness for a high school student can be measured in many ways, both subjective and objective. Eighteen is not some magical number that ensures such readiness. It could come earlier, or later, or not at all. Furthermore, college is not the only answer to what's next after high school. Programs for certification in trades like carpentry and plumbing, apprenticeship opportunities, work experience with management goals in mind, or the military, are all viable routes for independence and maturity. College isn't going anywhere.

Options in Public School—Early College High Schools

Early College High Schools (ECHS) emerged in 2002 with funding from the Bill & Melinda Gates Foundation. The goal to assist lower socioeconomic students (SES) and potential first-generation college students has been a commendable success. ECHS allow students to potentially graduate with an Associate's Degree at the same time they graduate with their high school diploma. ECHS serve a special purpose for low-income and other traditionally under-served students by offering tuition-free college credits (Berger et al., 2010; Haxton et al., 2016; McDonald & Farrell, 2012; Saenz & Combs, 2015). These students fare much better in early college high schools than they do in traditional education. Their degree attainment for under-served early college students reaches up to ten times that of under-served high school students who do not receive additional attention (Haxton et al., 2016). They are not prevalent in all areas of the country. Their success is not limited to low-SES students either. Earning college credits while still in high school can allow a future college student to take a broader range of classes at a university, since prerequisites will likely have been met, as well as graduating quicker and thus making a Bachelor's degree more affordable. Like all schools, they will vary in quality depending upon numerous factors over which a parent has virtually no control, but they are certainly a worthy consideration.

Options in Public School—Advanced Placement

Advanced Placement (AP), is a product of the College Board. The College Board is the mothership of all things related to college entrance tests. AP can be a great equalizer in some ways in that it provides an opportunity to be taught alongside other motivated learners and sit for an exam at the end of the year to prove your mastery of the topic. The ideal vision is that you will have a good teacher, you will master the material, and you will test well on the day of the AP exam, you will then likely be awarded college credit or advanced placement into higher-level classes at many colleges. While this entire year is spent teaching to a test, it can be a great experience for many students. One of the best perks of AP classes is the self-selection that takes place; specifically, there are less likely to be unmotivated learners slowing down the pace.

Conversely, you could take the equivalent college course and be able to prove yourself over multiple tests given over a semester and receive normal college credit. College credit from a community college will generally be accepted by a public university in the same state as the community college. Out of state and private universities have their own changing parameters of what credits they accept and how they apply them, however, it is typical that basic core freshman classes are transferable and credit awarded. The use of AP by colleges and universities also comes in and out of vogue over time, whereas sitting for a college class at the community college is generally more stable and reliable (see below).

Options in Public School—IB

International Baccalaureate (IB) programs are another potentially great option. IB programs are known to be writing intensive, which is a good thing generally, but can also require an inordinate amount of time from your student. Graduation from these programs are certainly more prestigious than a regular high school diploma, but the time and labor involved mean it's important to discuss thoroughly with your student first. Rigorous AP coursework and IB coursework may come with a significant time commitment and questionable payoff. Certainly, some kids excel on these paths. Others sacrifice a great deal of time, lose out on opportunities, and suffer some heartache from poor test results due to anxiety, illness, etc. If college acceptance to a highly selective university is a priority for you, then the value of IB vs. AP vs. DE is a conversation to be had with a college consultant. The changing paradigms of college admissions are too complex to discuss here. However, the proliferation of college consultants and books on the market certainly speak to that new reality (see below).

Private Schools

There are a plethora of private secular and parochial schools in the U.S. The philosophy, cost, and rate of success of each can vary greatly. Catholic schools have a long and well-documented history of excellence in education. Parochial schools do not necessarily require adherence to a religious tenet but certainly require respect for the practices of the school. Whereas one might think a private school would be more accommodating to your child's needs since you are writing a check each month, that may not be the case. Private schools may feel they have mastered how education should be and offer limited flexibility for those reasons; they may be too small to be able to practically effect a change in their system; or else, they may not want to accommodate one child for fear of opening the floodgates to more demanding parents. Research has found private schools to be more successful than public schools, but not as much as one might expect (see Chapter 2). It would be comforting to assume that writing a check means your child is getting a superior education, but again, there are too many variables to assume that is the case.

Charter Schools

There has been a growth in charter schools in recent years. Charter schools are unique in that they are free public schools that are privately owned. They are not in all states yet, but over 40. This is a prime example of the adage, YMMV (your mileage may vary), as there are so many variables to consider from school to school. One of the appeals of such schools is that they can be more dynamic as they are not part of a larger entity, such as a school district. Since these schools tend to have a specific vision, like STEM, they attract families who agree with their mission. This produces a more self-selecting group who shares the vision of the school and thus may be more motivated.

Teachers may or may not be certified and the school may or may not subscribe to the testing mandated for public schools. That fact may or may not be an issue though: YMMV. Because they are privately owned, they can choose to be less transparent in their decision making compared to a public school.

Boarding Schools

There are a few hundred boarding schools in the U.S., with most located in the northeast. The option to have your child live away for the school year is not one many families entertain or can afford. The pros and cons of boarding schools are lengthy and the stuff of many books, and are only mentioned here as a reference point.

Community College

Community college offers one of the best answers to educating your child. The cost differs based on numerous factors, with some districts offering free classes. Your student may flourish given the opportunity to manage themselves on a college campus, with help as needed. It can be empowering. Interacting with a more real-world gene pool than similarly-aged kids in your zip code area can be intellectually stimulating. And most of all, escaping the evaluation of an entire year of study in just a few hours during an AP exam, could be liberating.

Knowledge is power. As may be obvious from the above, community college can be, for many gifted students, the preferred option. However, obtaining entrance into community college has various protocols depending on where you live and the age and status of your child. Age discrimination is illegal and if the child has qualifying test scores via standardized tests such as the ACT, SAT, or the local community college tests, then it should not be an issue. Local homeschooling groups and private email loops, like Yahoo's College Confidential, provide a free forum to ask questions and obtain up to date information from parents in the trenches. We also discuss this further in Part 3.

College Consultants/Independent Educational Consultants

The free market proves time and time again that if there is a demand, businesses will meet that need. Self-checkout at grocery stores, kiosks at fast-food restaurants, and Uber everything, shows how the market meets the demand. In the same spirit, the college consultant business has taken off.

Applying for colleges, especially the more competitive ones, is much more complicated than it has been in the past. Professionals can take the mystery out of it. In fact, many parents and students are unfamiliar with how to search for colleges that will be a good fit academically, socially, and financially. The application process is not always straightforward and the financial aid process is undoubtedly complex. In fact, multiple financial aid forms can be required in a timely manner and can surprise and/or overwhelm the student and parent trying to make sure they have done everything. Consultants can minimize the mystery and provide insights all along the way.

Conclusion

There are many roads to explore when trying to do what is best for your child. Your local school may also be a great option. It may be your only option. Regardless, knowing there is more than one path to a great education should embolden you to think outside the walls of that brick and mortar building.

Have you ever wondered how many hours you expect your student to spend on schoolwork vs. social life vs. volunteering vs. family time vs. working vs. just life? These are also valid questions. Many students work the equivalent of two full-time jobs to get great grades, extracurriculars, volunteer hours, and accumulate accolades to pad an elite college dossier. Again, it is incredibly subjective as to the value of such things. While one motivated student can accomplish a great deal, a different student can be overwhelmed with the same pressures. The impact on their physical and mental health can be crippling. The number of students committing self-harm, taking all manner of legal and illegal drugs, and indulging in other risky behaviors in an attempt to cope with these pressures is soul-crushing. In addition, the cheating that goes on to ensure a high-grade point average in response to such pressures is horrendous. Parents and administrators are not immune from these crises either. Sadly, they can be part of the problem. Yet, we expect our young people to manage and flourish in these environments that often swarm with such hazards?

What is the best answer for your family? Remember, there are many roads to explore when trying to do what is best for your child. Your local school may also be a great option; it may be your only option. Regardless, knowing there is more than one path to a great education should embolden you to think outside the walls of that brick and mortar building.

References

Arum, R. (2011). *Academically Adrift: Limited Learning on College Campuses.* University of Chicago Press.

Department of Education, Institute of Education Sciences, (1992). *National Adult Literacy Survey*

Department of Education, Institute of Education Sciences, (2003). *National Assessment of Adult Literacy.*

Wainer, H. (2011). *Uneducated Guesses: Using Evidence to Uncover Misguided Education Policies.* Princeton University Press.

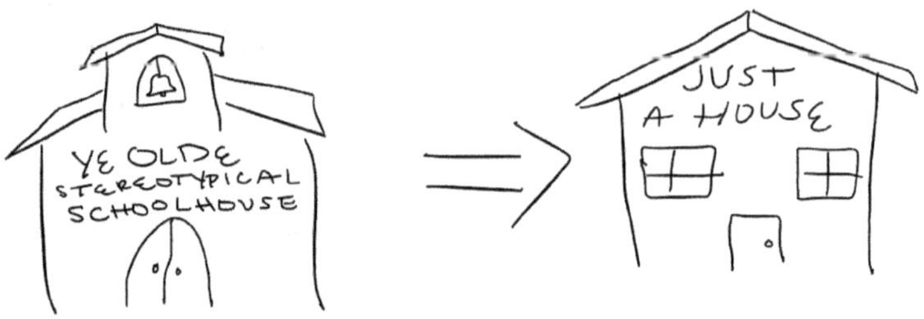

Looking Back with Myiesha: Schooling to Homeschooling

Our transition to homeschooling was gradual and unintended. When the children were in early elementary school, I recognized the need for summertime and holiday enrichment. At that time, I was not ready to dive into full-time homeschooling, but I was happy to enthusiastically enrich their educational experience. I realized that I did not have to pull them out of public school to homeschool: there was plenty of time to homeschool when my children weren't at school. By creating a personalized supplemental curriculum, my children enjoyed the very best I had to offer. Initially created as supplemental, out-of-school life lessons, "Taylored Curriculum" was our name for at-home education which quickly blossomed into a more strategic endeavor to fill the deficit that school left in their educational journey.

After reading what Malcolm Gladwell's book, *Outliers,* had to say about the disparities in achievement between children who had more structured summer learning opportunities vs. those who had "summer breaks," I really turned up the heat on the Taylored Curriculum in the summer of 2011. This was made easier by the fact that we were not a family of farmers with crops to harvest and bring to market—the main reason summer breaks were instituted in the first place!

Studies show that children from wealthy families keep learning over their summer breaks while children from poorer families often backslide (Alexander et al., 2007; Borman et al., 2005; Burkam et al., 2004). The difference lies both in wealth—wealthier parents can invest more time and money in their children— and in parenting styles—wealthier parents generally believe it is their duty to invest in their children's education and future, and are more likely to have the educational background to do so. More than half of the achievement gap between lower- and higher-income youth can be explained by unequal access to summer learning opportunities. As a result, low-income youth are less likely to graduate from high school or enter college (Alexander et al., 2007).

Taylored Curriculum was a lot of work, but it was entirely worth it. I spent hours/days/weeks in late spring scouring our local accommodations for educational, child-friendly activities that fit my various criteria. Emailing ranch owners who teach children to care for and ride horses, seeking out photography classes, learning to type, canvas painting, yoga, scrapbooking, swimming instruction, basketball camps, book clubs. We took a week off to be with visiting family and had a fabulous stay-cation learning how to be good hosts and the nuances of hospitality. We ate at nice restaurants and learned about etiquette and proper manners. We planned an extremely busy road trip where we saw many national monuments and practiced our social skills by interacting with public officials and politicians, all the while reading books and flashcards during the journey to help solidify and add perspective to the journey.

My impetus for pursuing this homeschool journey was Haley. We'd been blessed with great elementary school teachers. Yes, Haley had been in 7 schools in her 10 years on this earth, but each move was designed to remedy a specific undesirable situation. I finally realized that perhaps there wasn't a traditional school that would optimize Haley's potential in all areas, especially her natural aptitude for leadership. (The truth is that leadership is not as desirable an attribute as one might think in public school, where conformity is expected, encouraged, and occasionally enforced).

After moving to Texas, we were able to find a great elementary school: Haley's teachers were outstanding and strong advocates for their students. Sadly, while there were many positive attributes of this school, I became increasingly frustrated (as did the classroom teachers and school leadership) with the focus on the standardized exams. Further, the "new way" of teaching math was inflexible and stressful for many parents, students, and teachers. Haley went from being an enthusiastic math student to a struggling one, and we were powerless to customize or tailor her learning because the standardized exam (and methods of instruction) allowed no flexibility. Finally, although we advocated for her to be tested for the Gifted and Talented Program, we were told repeatedly that she was not eligible to be tested because testing was done in kindergarten only. Her teacher actually did not think highly of the program anyway, saying that it was a waste of time and interrupted the child's educational flow. "All they do is play with LEGOs and then when they get back they have missed important information."

After a relatively positive experience in elementary school, we were actually excited for intermediate school. That excitement quickly died out: I was not impressed with the lack of rigor in the curriculum, as I had anticipated more challenging and relevant academic programs at this level. In fifth grade, the teachers become more specialized and the students spent time in separate classes to learn different subjects. I was optimistic that my daughter would be challenged and thrive, but unfortunately, that was not our experience. Fifth grade was essentially a repeat of fourth grade. The focus was still on standardized testing. There was no room for teaching customization or individualization; the teachers were less personal and seemed to be under more stress. I was also annoyed by the limits placed on my parenting: for instance, if I wanted to go to the school and pick up my child and take her to lunch, an "excuse" was demanded. If we decided to take them on a business trip to see the world and have them miss a few days of school, we could expect letters from the district threatening to charge us with a crime and jeopardizing our professional licenses. This is *my* child and I was being treated like a criminally-negligent babysitter!

In fifth grade, it is not uncommon for the quintessential "mean girl drama" to present. In order to avoid being targeted, girls often morph into whatever they need to be to avoid being ostracized. For my daughter, this meant diminishing her intelligence and lowering her life expectations. The focus of school for her went from learning and loving her teacher to worrying about her social status in peer-groups. This was a huge distraction, and very disempowering to her. Throughout this fifth grade year, I watched my fiery, talkative, confident girl with a passionate love of learning transform into a passive, anxious, insecure girl who could never quite fully manipulate her personality to "fit in" (though not for a lack of trying, sadly). There was an abundance of other social issues present that further exacerbated this situation. There were emotionally disturbed friends—at this time it was a popular insult to tell people to "go kill themselves," and discussing one's most dramatic, possibly exaggerated suicidal desires was socially acceptable and encouraged within her age group. Teachers were frequently absent: there were so many "teacher training days" and allocated days off that, in any given week, there was a high probability that at least one of them would be absent, which disrupted the flow of the classroom and the students' ability to learn. As is a common issue, the testing was excessive, and all the teaching revolved around the tests. And—another common issue—bullying was rampant and had become an entirely new frontier with the dawn of social media.

So, I started wondering: Is there a part-time school that condenses the academic presentation and allows for flexibility through self-study that could tap into our Taylored Curriculum? Where we wouldn't be relegated to typical after-school hours, weekends, and school holidays and would have the ability to better bond with our children so we could be more effective life coaches and parents? The answer was two-fold: homes-chooling and college.

I made the decision to try something new: I pulled her out of school and enrolled her in a hybrid homeschool- university model of schooling (which we discuss at greater length in Part 3). When I asked her how she felt about this idea, her initial response was concern: "I'll be the new kid again and have no friends." One week later when one "friend" disowned her, and another got sent to an alternative school. I explained to her that childhood friendships are inherently unstable; I explained that families frequently move for jobs and opportunities and childhood friendships end. When we were little this was less common, but nowadays, adults find themselves relocating frequently, making the schoolyard friendships even more unpredictable. It was obvious she understood my message when a few days later she said this to me: "I realize that my friends aren't really my friends. I'm excited to spend more time with you and Dad instead, learning stuff so I'll actually be smart! It's so frustrating to try to make myself stupid so I don't stand out and get teased. None of the boys like smart girls. And I don't think I'm learning anything good at school."

After that, homeschooling flourished like never before, and we realized how far letting Haley go at her own pace could take her. We wanted school to work. We fought so hard and tried so many programs before suddenly I began to wonder what the point of it was at all. Were there really benefits to this system? Asking kids to sit still? Having short work periods and long breaks? Having pre-teens work out their psychosocial development together in a dysfunctional environment? Leaving our kids with other adults instead of having them at home? In trusting in this blindly, how much had I taken for granted, and how many opportunities had I ignored? The further we went into our homeschooling journey, the better I felt about our choice to take a leap of faith and trust in ourselves and our kids.

References

Alexander, K. L., Entwisle, D. R., Olson, L. S. (2007). Lasting consequences of the summer learning gap. *American Sociological Review, 72*(2), 167-180. doi:10.1177/000312240707200202

Borman, G. D., Benson, J., & Overman, L. T. (2005). Families, schools, and summer learning. *The Elementary School Journal, 106*(2), 131-150. doi:10.1086/499195

Burkam, D. T., Ready, D. D., Lee, V. E., & LoGerfo, L. F. (2004). Social-class differences in summer learning between kindergarten and first grade: Model specification and estimation. *Sociology of Education, 77*(1), 1-31. doi:10.1177/003804070407700101

Gladwell, M. (2008). *Outliers, The Story of Success.* New York: Little, Brown and Company.

Looking Back with Nancy: Kinder to College

Through our two months in half-day Kindergarten, we joyfully and blissfully homeschooled old-school style, around the kitchen table, and on the couch, and with our trusty dry erase/ chalkboard easel. Since Noel was already reading chapter books at this time, the library was our main resource. So many colorful, interesting, silly, profound, and amazing books to choose from. Many wonderful memories were forged as we cuddled on the couch to share the joy of reading and the resulting conversations—it warmed my momma's heart. Noel would also draw and dance about while I read. I would ask her questions to assure she was following the storyline and engaged; and she was! We didn't need to prepare for a quiz, spelling, or vocabulary test, etc. No, we just enjoyed the story. So much learning is happening simultaneously, but little kiddos don't know that. It was simply a joy. Talking about the book, wondering where the story was going, imagining ourselves as the characters, conversations about the moral of the story and its plot twists. All this, while enjoying the bright colors, interesting characters, beautiful artwork, and words words words to discover. The bonding between parent and child over a shared experience is a pivotal part of a healthy relationship—and that bond is so much easier when made at home and without the pressures of mandated testing lurking around the corner.

Back in the early 2000s, we were blessed with a brick and mortar homeschool store in our area that offered new and used curricula and even a few classes for homeschool kids. We progressed forward with the insights of other parents who were further along the journey than us. We were also at ease knowing that we were not committing to homeschooling her all the way through high school, but simply one year at a time, which is an oft-used mantra for homeschooling. So, the pressure of believing that I would be her only teacher until college was absent and absolutely untrue. Probably the second most common mantra of homeschoolers is "don't try to do public-school at home." You have so much more flexibility than the school does. You certainly could buy one all-encompassing curriculum and stick with that, but so many amazing choices await. The cornucopia of options available to homeschoolers is an embarrassment of riches.

Since Noel was gifted and knowing I had no official pass-fail scenario at the end of the school year, it was easy enough to go to a homeschool store and just shop. I sought out curricula that were most interesting and would be engaging but not overwhelming (for either of us). There was even a little play area in the store and I would plop her there to play with the fresh puzzles or books while I browsed. I would walk over and ask her opinion on occasion and also ask academic questions to best judge what level I thought she was capable of. One of the best things ever about homeschooling is the ability to accelerate without drama. Or conversely, catch up without stigma. They just do the work they are capable of doing well. They don't have to do it perfectly, but it needs to be hard enough to make them think, just not so hard that they struggle constantly. Schools have a mountain of paperwork and protocols that make such things extraordinarily complex and potentially painful for the child.

Do you think a chess expert would enjoy being forced to only play checkers for a year? Probably not. Similarly, finding the skills your child excels at, and then subsequently letting them excel, is much more fulfilling than forcing them to painstakingly go through every protocol just because other kids might need it.

We forged ahead with the aid of the library, homeschooling co-ops, homeschooling cafeteria-style schools—both local and online, homeschooling friends, actual curricula we bought and used: some curricula we bought and found was too easy, was not a good fit, or simply never got around to use…Life was good. We set our own hours and could spontaneously visit the park on especially beautiful days. Museums and time with friends were also easier to arrange. Freedom, it is indeed awesome.

We had been homeschooling since October of 2004 with much joy and passion and minimal hiccups. We had met local friends through homeschool classes, and co-ops. We had other homeschooling families to share the journey with, although not necessarily as gifted as Noel, they were extraordinarily lovely. We found a Girl Scout troop, piano teacher, enrichment classes, homeschooling PE options, and friends, as we breezed through material and enjoyed the journey. All was right with the world.

Teaching elementary math was one of the easiest subjects. A few used laminated posters from the homeschool store and my dry erase board were all I needed. As it turned out, she did not need repetition ad nauseum to learn math. We cranked through the equivalent of six years of math during that Kindergarten year. The only curriculum I bought was a fifth grade Saxon math book. Saxon is the educational equivalent of the old reliable truck your grandpa had that keeps on running with torn up seats and faded paint, but still gets the job done. It is not pretty or especially engaging, but it is effective. That was Saxon math for us. One of those pearls of wisdom you hear at the right time in your life, came from a mom who was part of a homeschooling co-op we were in. This co-op only met every other Friday morning. There were three one-hour classes you could choose for your kid, and given her academic prowess, we focused on non-academic choices—PE, art, music. It was an easy opportunity to meet other families, make friends, and just enjoy life. No mandated attendance, no grades to earn, just learning to exist with others, in an extraordinarily loving and relaxed environment. For us, as Christians, it was affirming for our faith as well.

One of these moms—an attorney actually—mentioned in passing that you do not have to do every problem, in every section, for every chapter with Saxon math. Wait, what? This powerhouse publisher may not know my child's needs better than me? I do not have to bow down to everything and everyone more learned than I? It is possible that I may not be as utterly ill-equipped to educate my own flesh and blood than I fear I may be? That was more than helpful to hear. This information proved exponentially helpful (see the math reference there). It was life-changing. From then on, I respected curriculum I chose, but did not worship it. I used the best and skipped the rest. That was a huge leap forward for us.

The beauty of a gifted child is that they typically learn faster than the average student or certainly get things on a deeper meaning than average. Repetition ad nauseum can be unmotivating, can engrain mistakes, and can simply suck the joy out of learning. But when you are learning with 20-30+ other kids, you have to average all their needs out. Slower learners struggle. Faster learners are bored. That middle part of the Bell

Curve is where the public school aims. It is a flawed system, at best. More likely, a broken system; again, this is the stuff of many books and theories.

When we pulled Noel out of Kindergarten, all of our friends assumed something drastic had happened. Many questions were asked. I found myself in the same quandary I had with Conner back at the Color Center! I certainly do not want to diminish Noel's abilities, but nor do I want anyone to feel bad. This is sadly the lot for academically gifted kids: it is often awkward to be 100% honest about their abilities. If you moved your kid up to a sports league because they had the skill, it would be heralded as awesome for your gifted athletic kiddo, but academically, you risk being labeled as elitist. Sigh.

At age 8, I booked an appointment with an educational diagnostician/Ph.D. at the University of North Texas. The $250 for that test was another life-changing event. Noel was always an outgoing kiddo and not easily intimidated, so with no preparation or even an explanation, I told her she was going to meet with someone so I could just see how she was doing with our homeschooling. After the testing, the Ph.D. led her back to me and stated, "You didn't tell me how smart she was." In my mind, I'm thinking, "Well, that would be rude, wouldn't it? But, also, what am I supposed to do about that?" She tells me it will take a week or so to get the report, but in the interim I should check out the Davidson Institute for Talent Development. I had absolutely no idea what she was talking about.

The Davidson Institute for Talent Development is the amazing philanthropic work of Bob and Jan Davidson. Their groundbreaking 2005 book, *Genius Denied: How to Stop Wasting Our Brightest Young Minds* details the crisis of education for the gifted in America. "...gifted students spending their days in classrooms learning little beyond how to cope with boredom as they "relearn" material they've already mastered years before. This lack of challenge leads to frustration, underachievement, and even failure. Some gifted students become severely depressed. At a time when our country needs a deep intellectual talent pool, the squandering of these bright young minds is a national tragedy." The Institute provides a variety of free services for PG kids: Profoundly Gifted children.

Wait, what? Profoundly Gifted? There are *levels* of giftedness? My baby girl?

That one little comment spun our world. I didn't really believe it though. Surely, she wasn't that smart? She was doing algebra at 8, but that is just a fluke, right? Who would I talk to about this? What was I to do exactly? So many questions.

I might note that levels of giftedness is yet another topic without definitive consensus. Some sources break giftedness down as: mild, moderate, highly, exceptional, profound and beyond, with varying test scores to quantify each. Others see this as hair-splitting or question the implications of these levels. We can conclude that "levels" of giftedness is not an exact science.

One of the best things about being a part of the Davidson Young Scholar (DYS) Program is the ability to meet other families in your area. I was not shy about reaching out to everyone near (and not so near) to me if they had a girl around Noel's age. An opportunity to share stories and learn from others on your same journey is priceless. It worked out that we began homeschooling on Fridays with a group of gifted homeschoolers, of which five were DYS too. The other parents brought fantastic skill sets and/or connections to lead this co-op. What did I bring? The only girl Young Scholar. Those were amazing days filled with unending lessons in academic achievement, friendship, and fun. Spending time with parents who had figured out homeschooling profoundly gifted kids better than I was another life-changing development.

A hilarious contrast in our life happened one day back when Noel was about 10. We had a Girl Scout meeting in the morning and then we all went to the neighborhood park to hang out afterwards. The girls, who were varying ages (which is often the norm in a homeschooling troop), played, talked, and had a game of Hide and Seek. Low-key fun. We then had lunch in the car (fast food—as I sadly was not that type of homeschool mom that had a garden and was into canning or knitting sweaters) and drove across the metroplex for a park day with our DYS guy friends at a nature reserve. These kids (also of varying ages) played a game of Civilization, as it were, at the park. Civilization is a game where you take on the role of a ruler and build cities and products to try and create an empire. They each decided which area of the park was their land and discussed what products their land would develop. Noel had seen her Dad play this game on the computer, but she had not played it herself. The guys, on the other hand, were old hands. I was a little worried that she would not be able to manage this type of vibe with an all guy gang compared to the Girl Scout gals. I'm the mom, I worry. When all was said and done, she said she had a great time and did well in the game as her land produced American Girl dolls and the guys would buy her product and then blow them up! Too funny! This is an example of gifted kids—they don't always have existential conversations or discuss quantum physics, they just play slightly more complex games with a better vocabulary most of the time.

A not-so-hilarious example of our life involved my utter incompetence at math. My basic understanding of mathematics was sadly abysmal. All I knew what what I had been taught—algebra, geometry, and calculus. That is like saying that all art is just classical music, ballet, and sculpture. So much ignorance on my part. We had used Saxon, Singapore Math for a bit, and then a homeschool curriculum that involved a lot of memorization. Believe it or not, at age seven, Noel memorized all the prime numbers up to 1000, and was able to circle them out of all the numbers 1 through 1000 in two minutes, perfectly. For such a skill, she earned a special ribbon. Turns out ribbons are even cooler than stickers when you are seven. That curriculum was challenging and self-paced. Perfect. Noel had jumped through the hoops to qualify for high school algebra at age eight. We worked through the algebra together. It was an awesome yet somewhat sorry day for me when she could factor polynomials faster and more accurately than myself.

But it was soon after this time that we began to homeschool with our profoundly gifted friends. Our world grew. We learned about Abstract Algebra, writing proofs, math competitions, etc. We learned of amazing lectures by the Teaching Company's Great Courses series. An early favorite was "The Joy of Thinking." Various professors would discuss a math concept for 20-30 minutes and explore it for the beauty of the math. Again, no test, just the amazing wonder of it all. They would talk about Pascal's Triangle, Fibonacci numbers, and Mobius Strips, for example. Simply beautiful. There were 24 lectures and I would let her choose which one she wanted to watch, sometimes watching one multiple times. One of my favorite memories was her sheepishly asking to watch "The Sexiest Rectangle" at age 8. Spoiler Alert—it is the golden ratio, and a known measurement of beauty across cultures and time. But that sheepish grin as she said the word "sexiest", for what I hoped was the first time, was priceless. And as a bonus, we both learned alot about geometry, ratios, and culture in that lecture. Dr. Arthur Benjamin, who was the prof on many of those lessons, would end up being a speaker at a conference we attended the next year. I do not believe she loved him like I loved David Cassidy of The Partridge Family era, but he was a rock star to her nonetheless.

Most kids are friends with the kids they go to school with, which are the kids in their neighborhood and/or kids they know from shared interests like church, Scouts, etc. Those kids are generally the same age and grade. As homeschoolers for most of Noel's youth, we had to make the call over and over again as to whether to align Noel with age peers or academic peers. We opted for a little from column A and a little from column B with various levels of success and failure. Girl Scouts, church youth groups and programs, theater, art classes, robotics and math competitions, all-girl rock bands, homeschool co-ops, online classes, volunteering, etc. was where we spent our time when not homeschooling at home.

When she was twelve and enrolled in a public magnet high school (albeit for only one semester), not everyone wanted her in high school groups. Was that because of normal boy/girl conflict, bullying, girl drama, gifted vs. non-gifted, or just a totally normal not-everybody-gets-along-with everybody-all-the-time reality. Who knows? Those are all personal and completely subjective decisions parents and kids make all the time. Acceleration just adds another component to the mix. Like life in general, you do the best with what you know at the time, then hopefully when you know better, you do better. This is a lesson to be learned as early in life as possible—do not assume malice when ignorance is a possible alternative. Why teenagers would reject a pre-teen likely has all sorts of layers to it—some can be addressed and remedied, some not. Some kids crave peer acceptance more than academic appropriateness. Other kids would rather be alone with Shakespeare or Hawking than feel awkward with a group of kids their age talking about what Nike socks are in fashion or similar inane chit chat. Ideally, kids will be comfortable enough in their own skin to manage both situations and strong enough in their character to be true to themselves. Yet, we all fall short of "ideal" much of the time.

Even before we got pregnant, it was always Noel's dad that wanted us to homeschool. He was not a fan of the public education he had received, even though he attended way better schools than me over the course of our K-12 education. We lived in a good district, I never thought we would need to homeschool, and to be embarrassingly honest, I always envisioned my unborn child as the future Most Popular, Valedictorian, Homecoming Queen, Head Cheerleader, athletic rock star, and musical prodigy along with all the other accolades I had craved as a teen. Homeschooling seemed wholly antithetical to those goals. By the Grace of God, I quickly realized how absolutely ridiculous I had been, and embraced the individual who was my child, once she finally arrived.

As social a creature as Noel was and is, academic mediocrity and its meaner evil twin, slow-paced academic mediocrity, felt so stagnant that the situation became untenable. So our time in public school lasted only one semester—twice the length of her Kindergarten experience (lest we be seen as quitters). Intellectual vitality is a terrible thing to waste. As homeschoolers, we worked hard to maintain social connections, driving 50 miles one way one, two, or three times a week, to find that rarest of breeds: academic and age peers. Contrary to the stereotype of tiger parents, we tried to slow Noel down, but it was her desire and drive that moved us forward academically, not any pushing on our part. We certainly had no idea that when we pulled her from Kindergarten at age five, we would watch her be hooded for her Ph.D. 14 years later. But wow, what a ride!

Chapter 6
Homeschooling Misconceptions

Misconceptions about homeschooling plague the Western education system, and prevent us from promoting a proven successful educational strategy. Here we address some of the most common myths about home-ed. And a quick note: we don't use many academic citations in this book because this is more a collection of stories than a research paper, but in this chapter we've included them just to show there is no way to deny the facts!

The Myth: Homeschooling isn't a real education.

Ray (2010) found just the opposite. Homeschool students have higher achievement test scores than their public counterparts. There are actually two ways to explain this: it could be that smarter students choose to homeschool more often, which would mean that it's not the advantage of homeschooling, but the inherent smartness of the child; it could also be due to the actual nature of homeschooling itself. While Ray's research does indicate homeschooling is utilized by the unserved gifted students of America, it found that homeschooled students outperformed their public peers whether or not their parents predicted they would. More simply put, a parent who pulled their kid out of public school because of unmet, advanced academic needs would likely have knowledge of higher achievement scores beforehand; in this study, parents who had no previous knowledge of their students' high test scores *still* produced students with better results through homeschooling. Homeschooling isn't just good for the smartest kids in class!

The Myth: Parents homeschool because they don't trust public education, particularly for religious reasons.

Maybe in the past, but that's not what drives families to choose homeschooling nowadays. When surveyed, parents homeschooling their children often expressed a desire to be more involved in their child's education; their beliefs about public education were less relevant (Green & Hoover-Dempsey, 2007). We might add, however, that many have good reason to have lost trust in public education. While religion may be a factor—or just a bonus—for some homeschoolers, the research indicates it is the defining factor for only a small minority.

The Myth: Homeschoolers are socially inept, awkward, or otherwise "weird."

Maybe! Weirdos are everywhere! I met plenty in public school, and I met plenty at homeschool co-ops. It's not the easiest thing to scientifically measure and report on a population's oddities because "awkwardness" or "weirdness" can be quite subjective. Regardless, research has found a plethora of fascinating results on the social aptitude and psychological adjustment of homeschoolers. But why parrot it back when the original resource puts it so perfectly? Here's the abstract from Medlin's (2013) review of the research:

> *"The research indicates that homeschooling parents expect their children to respect and get along with people of diverse backgrounds, provide their children with a variety of social opportunities outside the family, and believe their children's social skills are at least as good as those of other children. What homeschooled children think about their own social skills is less clear. Compared to children attending conventional schools,*

> *however, research suggests that they have higher quality friendships and better relationships with their parents and other adults. They are happy, optimistic, and satisfied with their lives. Their moral reasoning is at least as advanced as that of other children, and they may be more likely to act unselfishly. As adolescents, they have a strong sense of social responsibility and exhibit less emotional turmoil and problem behaviors than their peers. Those who go on to college are socially involved and open to new experiences. Adults who were homeschooled as children are civically engaged and functioning competently in every way measured so far. An alarmist view of homeschooling, therefore, is not supported by empirical research. It is suggested that future studies focus not on outcomes of socialization but on the process itself."*

I think Medlin (2013) pretty much shuts the book on that one. There is more to understand, from an empirical view, on how to facilitate effective socialization in homeschooling. Sadly, the definition of "socialization" is weak…and I've yet to see anyone present evidence on the quality of socialization in public or even private brick-and-mortar schools.

A few other myths include:

Parents should be certified as teachers to be qualified to homeschool.

Homeschooling parents with teacher certifications produce students with *lower* scores than their uncertified counterparts (Ray, 2009). Ouch.

Homeschoolers aren't going to be wanted by colleges.

Homeschoolers are more likely to attend (and graduate) college (Cogan, 2010; US Census Bureau, 2003). They enter with more credits and have higher SAT and ACT scores (Cogan, 2010). A little over 74% of college admissions board members expected homeschool graduates to perform just as well or better than high school graduates in their first year at college (Jones & Gloeckner, 2004).

Well, they won't do well in college then.

They're actually more likely to graduate college, as well (Cogan, 2010; US Census Bureau, 2003). College students who were homeschooled beforehand are demographically similar to their peers, and yet earn higher tertiary calculus grades (Wilkens et al., 2015). And as Drenovsky & Cohen (2012) so eloquently summarized, "previously homeschooled students do not present with any significant differences in self-esteem than [other college] students who were traditionally educated, and are more likely to succeed academically and less likely to experience depression than their [college] classmates."

At the very least, states need to regulate homeschooling or we're going to end up with kids who can't read!

States with high regulations on homeschooling do not see better results than those with more educational freedom (Ray, 2009).

Well, I don't like it! I think it's bad and strange!

That's perfectly fine. Maintaining your beliefs in the face of significant empirical evidence to the contrary is your right as an American, and something humans are very good at—if not designed specifically to do.

As to why these misconceptions exist, it is due to a combination of misinformation and a lack of actual information. We fear what we do not understand. Research from the 1990s and further back does indicate there was a time when homeschoolers were mainly a religious minority with lower reading and math ability. Of course, as we saw in Chapter 1, there was a time when uneducated parents had no choice but to homeschool their children, because they couldn't afford schooling. However, the figures just don't support this today. What they do support is the advocation of homeschooling as a valuable resource for students of all backgrounds to set themselves apart. Clearly this message is spreading because we are seeing anywhere from a 7% to 15% increase in homeschooling families annually (Hill, 2000). The truth is that I wish homeschooling wasn't necessary. It's a solution to a radically unfair problem: we offer a "free" public system under the guise that it is a decent option for everyone; we provide families with resources if they cannot work with the public system in very specific situations, but not in others; we expect families who are not supported to figure everything out themselves, and then we start demonizing them and believing rumors that they are religious nuts, that they won't be properly educated, or that they're just too picky.

If you pull your kid out of public school and send them to a ritzy private school because you think they'll get something better there, no one bats an eyelid. But if you pull them out and *don't* send them to private school because you can't afford it, or because you're not of the same religion as the local private school, or because you are the same religion but prefer education to stay secular, or because their disciplinary system is too harsh, or because their disciplinary system is too lenient, or because it is a single-gender private school and you would prefer your child learn in a co-ed environment, or because they don't provide accommodations for your child's learning disability, or because they don't provide accommodations for your child's physical disability, or because they refuse to allow grade-skipping or advanced work of any kind, or because they don't have the extracurriculars your child craves, or because the dress code is restrictive and sexist, or because the cafeteria isn't allergy-safe, or because your child would be a racial minority there, or because you are concerned about bullying and peer pressure, or because there is no private school near you, or because you simply think it's overpriced...suddenly, you have done your child some great disservice by homeschooling instead of compromising. Well, I am here to tell you the truth: homeschooling, as much as I wish it wasn't necessary, *is* a safe and effective option for turning any kind of student into a healthy, happy, educated adult.

References

Cogan, M. F. (2010). Exploring academic outcomes of homeschooled students. *Journal of College Admission, 208*, 18-25.

Drenovsky, C. K. & Cohen, I. (2012). The impact of homeschooling on the adjustment of college students. *International Social Science Review, 87*(1), 19-34.

Duvall, S. F., Delquadri, J. C., & Ward, D. L. (2004). A preliminary investigation of the effectiveness of homeschool instructional environments for students with Attention-Deficit/Hyperactivity Disorder. *School Psychology Review, 33*(1), 140-158.

Green, C. L. & Hoover-Dempsey, K. V. (2007) Why do parents homeschool? A systematic examination of parental involvement. *Education and Urban Society, 39*(2), 264-285. doi:10.1177/0013124506294862

Jones, P. & Gloeckner, G. (2004) A study of admission officers' perceptions and attitudes toward homeschool students. *The Journal of College Admission, 185*. 12-21.

Medlin, R. G. (2013). Homeschooling and the question of socialization revisited. *Peabody Journal of Education, 88*(3), 284-297. doi:10.1080/0161956X.2013.796825

Ray, B.D. (2010). Academic achievement and demographic traits of homeschool students: A nationwide study. *Academic Leadership, 8*(1), 1-32.

Wilkens, C. P., Wade, C. H., Sonnert, G., & Sadler, P. M. (2015). Are homeschoolers prepared for college calculus? *Journal of School Choice, 9*(1), 30-48. doi:10.1080/15582159.2015.998963

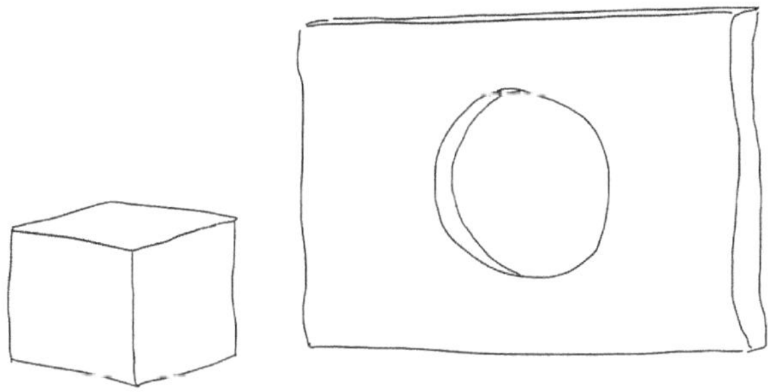

Looking Back with Haley: Our Reasons for Homeschooling

We decided to homeschool for two main reasons: public school was lacking in academic rigor, and I was obsessed with trying to fit in. My mother watched me diminish myself in an effort to have friends and be more palatable to boys that were intimidated by my intelligence and strong personality. That, combined with the fact that the school district refused to evaluate me for entry into the Gifted and Talented program, helped my parents realize that my needs were not going to be adequately met by a mass-produced educational model.

From kindergarten through 4th grade I had straight A's, was an enthusiastic student, and enjoyed school. Once I hit 5th grade my grades started to fall and instead of getting As, I brought home mostly Bs with little effort. When my mom tried to motivate me to try just a little bit harder to get that A, I explained to her that I was fine with Bs because I didn't stand out, and didn't have to work for them. This caused my mom a degree of distress because she felt she was watching school steal my love for learning and curiosity about the world.

Additionally, my parents did not like that teachers focused their instruction all year on STAAR preparation with the sole purpose of getting the class to do well on the STAAR test (a standardized state test). The week-long test period would become a very stressful time for us filled with chaos and anxiety. For instance, for the math portion they were teaching us long division using boxes and pictures, rather than classic, standard, normal long division. My mom tried to step in and teach me the correct way, but the teacher didn't appreciate it and strongly discouraged her. There was a bit of a fight which ended with my mother opting me out of the STAAR exam so, as she explained to the school staff "my test score wouldn't bring down the school average." Apparently, there were components of the STAAR exam that evaluated the process in which a solution was obtained in arithmetic, and not just whether the student understood how to get the correct answer. This meant that while I had the ability to solve the math problems and get the correct answer if I didn't do it *their* way, it would be marked incorrect. The frustrating thing was that after the test was finished in 5th grade, all the desks from our classroom were removed, and my classmates and I were left to sleep, joke around, and play in tents for the entirety of the school day. My parents didn't think that was a great use of my time in school, and neither did I.

When my parents made the decision to homeschool me, they took me to a psychologist for a learning evaluation in an effort to see how I best received information, and to ascertain any learning differences that needed special attention. When my psychologist's report revealed that my IQ was in the profoundly gifted range, my parents talked to me about how school would never be able to accommodate me. I remember having insight into my situation and understanding that their observations were true. I had some friends who were in a constant state of trying to "escape school" (that's literally what skipping school was called) through the chain-link fence, so they could go to

Burger King and socialize. I did not want to do that, but I didn't want to be left out either. I was struggling internally with what I knew I should be doing, and what I felt I needed to do in order to not be totally ostracized by schoolmates. When my mom suggested homeschooling, it offered another option that relieved the anxiety I felt.

I often get the question: "What would you say to students who are trying to 'find themselves' or 'find their own path in education'?"

I would remind them that our life journeys are individual endeavors and there is no predetermined path to find. You don't just find a paved path of education with a sign next to it with your name on it. Nor do you find a pre-formed shell of your body waiting for you when you turn a certain age where you can say "Hey look, I finally found myself!" That's not how life works. You must be willing to do the proverbial work. You cut the vines, trim the trees, and pave the road yourself. You make a path where there was none.

For parents who are trying to help their children create their own unique paths, I would offer this quote from a comment someone made to me on a radio interview, "Don't prepare the path for your child, prepare your child for the path." You are not your child. Your child has a separate life purpose and an individual path to follow. If you can help them learn how to develop and harness their own gifts, they will be uniquely poised to share those gifts with the world. If you show them how to trust their own insights and intuitions when navigating the world, they won't be so easily swayed from their self-determined destination.

Looking Back with Noel: Reflections on my "Socialization"

I look back on my social life throughout my whole life with pride. I never got the impression that homeschooling made my social life harder or smaller or less valuable, it simply made it more intentional. Early college did make my social life stranger, and I suppose it was harder, but it's difficult to quantify with no other experience to compare it to. Who's to say that a young girl in college will get along with their classmates any better or worse than she would with high schoolers? It's not as if a child who is ready for college at fourteen is usually the kind of child who thrives socially in a traditional high school.

As a young child, I was probably the closest to being popular I would ever get in my life. I was always trying to make everyone laugh, and it usually worked. Between Girl Scouts, basketball, 4-H, math club, chess club, robotics team, church, and all sorts of homeschool co-ops, I had a variety of social resources and friends from nearly every walk of life. I had friends from that stereotypical group of Christian homeschoolers who were sheltered and conservative, I had friends who went to public school, I had friends who went to private school, and I had friends who were radically accelerated through their homeschooling. Sure, I didn't have many friends who could provide everything I was looking for: I had very smart friends who were all boys, I had fun girlfriends but they went to public school, I had homeschooled friends but they weren't ready for the complex conversations I wanted to have. But I think this applies to most people, if I'm honest. We each have a friend or group of friends who suit each of our interests, and the more we can align with one person in terms of background, beliefs, and hobbies, the better we are going to get along with them on average.

I went to a traditional high school for one semester and that was my lowest point socially. School took away most of my time, therefore impeding my ability to engage in social activities outside school, and my classmates became my only social resource. But they weren't a great social resource. I had a few decent friends, but they never treated me like "one of them" since I was 12 at the time. It was also stressful dealing with the very mature and dark problems of dysfunctional 14-year-olds. Say what you will about being sheltered by homeschooling, but 12 was a bit young for me to deal with issues like drugs, STDs, teen pregnancy, incarceration, gangs, and suicide. Then again, I think 14 is a bit young for that too.

My high school only had 100 students as it was a first-year program. I was certainly bullied, but it was not overwhelmingly aggressive, as is the case with so many students. I found the teasing to be mostly lame, but it was funny when teenaged guys (14, I would guess) asked if I still got a "Happy Meal", since I was 12. I could honestly say no, as we didn't go to McDonald's, we were a Wendy's family. I enjoyed them being annoyed that I wasn't annoyed. They did almost hit the nail on the head though when they asked if I still rode in a car seat, as I had only recently been allowed to sit in the front seat.

Going to community college threw a wrench in the works to an extent. I didn't have much of a desire to be friends with the grown adults in my classes at thirteen. I did have a few acquaintances and those connections were valuable. Once again, I was interacting with people from all different walks of life. It was informative and invigorating. It's not often that a group of people that diverse in age and beliefs get to interact as equals. But I was still not making any friends there, and I also struggled more to make friends my own age, as they tended to find me unrelatable since I was in college. I became a bit less of a human and a bit more of a novelty. I spent more time suppressing my intelligence and accomplishments, and when I failed to do so, it tended to be detrimental to any new relationships forming. Thankfully, I had old friends who were still supportive of me, and of course, my advanced friends were understanding.

As for full-time college, I moved across the state so I had to "start from scratch," but I have so many amazing memories from this time. I joined a science fiction club that involved working at a comic convention, tons of movie nights and girls' events, gaming tournaments, study groups, and working a concession stand at sporting events. I was in a political organization, which was an important part of developing my beliefs and independence, and perhaps a bit of teenage rebellion. I even wrote for the school's satirical newspaper, which was an absolute blast and one of the most unique experiences of my life. So, I don't appreciate anyone saying that early college robbed me of the "college experience." I didn't do things that most college students do; I did things that most college students will never get to do. The vast majority of the things I "missed out" on, I will still be able to do in my 20s, even if I wasn't a college student then. Of course, it wasn't typical, if it had been I never would've gone on *Who Wants to Be a Millionaire*, among the other great opportunities acceleration has brought. Although I'm glad I got a decent social experience out of college, that was gravy compared to getting a quality education.

People ask me what I think my life would be like if I hadn't skipped any grades, or if I regret my decisions. I guess the diplomatic answer is to list all the great reasons why I did what I did, to justify myself to every passing stranger who asks me such a deeply personal question. I guess the aggressive answer is to ask them if they regret having kids, or marrying their partner, or taking their current job, so they understand that it's not helpful or kind to scrutinize my life like that. But the accurate answer is simply that I don't know or care how my life would be different. It's a waste of my time to regret what I can't change. My assumption is that if I had stayed behind, I would've survived for the most part but met the fate of the majority of those who ignore their need for acceleration: lower social skills, lower self-esteem, greater maladjustment.

I have a Doctorate. I have great friends. I have hobbies I love. I have a promising career path I am following, and so much more. Most of all, I have no regrets.

Chapter 7
Homeschooling and Special Populations

The Intellectually Gifted Learner

Defining the term "gifted" is controversial and difficult—you may as well ask "what is love?" and you'll probably get further with that pursuit. We'll give the word "gifted" a go, but (spoiler alert) there is no definitive, universal answer. The National Association for Gifted Children (NAGC) defines gifted children as those whose ability is significantly above the norm for their age and notes that this may manifest in one or more domains, such as intellectual, creative, artistic, leadership, or in some other specific academic field. It is common to consider those who score in the top 10% on standardized tests as gifted. However, the high intelligence society MENSA requires test-takers to score in the top 2% from the multiple IQ tests they accept. Some people subdivide the gifted to help identify specific needs in this diverse group. For example, The Davidson Institute for Talent Development is the leading non-profit organization for children who score in the 99.9th percentile on specific achievement and/or intelligence tests; they call this group the "profoundly gifted." The Triple Nine Society has slightly higher cutoffs than Davidson.

For many parents, the most important factor is how their school district defines giftedness. Schools have varying cutoffs and protocols for entry into their gifted and talented programs. Some schools require teacher referrals and in-house testing. Others will accept outside sources.

It is reasonable to conclude that some gifts are obvious, whereas other giftedness requires more digging. For example, do we need to be shown measurements to decide whether Serena Williams is gifted at tennis? Stephen Hawking at physics? Robin Williams at comedy? Beethoven at music? Or could it be that these individuals merely worked hard to master their craft? What about the girl who is bored out of her mind and makes minimal grades, but is capable of so much more? Or the boy who gets 100% but has to work for hours every night for those results? What if the child is twice-exceptional and their giftedness is being masked by dyslexia (which causes difficulties in reading), dysgraphia (which causes difficulties in writing), dyscalculia (which causes difficulties in math), or another condition? And sadly, it is known that race and SES interact with one's likelihood to be identified as gifted in school. Categorizing giftedness is an imperfect science and a complicated endeavor.

Due to the asynchronous nature of gifted children, their intellectual abilities and interests may be hugely disparate. Homeschooling allows the parent to accommodate this. In homeschooling the gifted student, the goal is to maintain many options open to your child for as long as possible. One example of this is the ability to delay one topic of study until the child is ready for it rather than teaching it en masse as public education has to. Another is acceleration. Acceleration to find appropriate level material is easy, yet you do not have to commit to those grade levels for other purposes. For example, your child can be in a sports league based on age and continue academic work at a higher level.

There are various ways of accommodating this. An excellent option is to select college-level curricula and work through it until college-level proficiency is demonstrated and then either test out of the class via CLEP (College Level Examination Program) or to take a college course and get a letter grade. This is beneficial because it cuts out the middleman from AP SAT Subject Test bureaucracy. However, please note that the student can also sit for these exams if necessary to legitimize and validate a homeschool transcript to seek entry into an elite university that may require these exams.

Children of Color

Our current system of mass education was established to shape the minds of young citizens, to instill an allegiance to country, and to produce factory workers with the basic skills to contribute to mass production. Given that integration and equal access to quality education were an afterthought of the education system, challenges to children of color run especially deep. It is an institution infused with damaging negative implicit biases, stereotype biases, misrepresentation, and erasure of curricular content. Students of color are less likely than their white counterparts to be assigned gifted enrichment. Black boys are disciplined more for exhibiting age-appropriate behavior; black girls experience significant disparate punishment and school office referrals.

Further, any parent of a child of color knows that it can be a struggle to engender a love for learning and appreciation of school when outward appearances supersede internal ideas and interests: A child may not think they are different—because in their own mind they are not that different—yet they are constantly reminded that they are different; this can create a complicated internal conflict that is difficult to resolve. It is human nature to be apprehensive, if not outright afraid of things unfamiliar. Therefore, a child that is an overwhelming minority within a classroom or school is often ostracized. This type of negative socialization, combined with the stark lack of diversity in leadership and teaching staff in most American schools, is counter-productive to learning and achieving academic excellence.

Homeschooling children of color allows the parent to incorporate into the curriculum a variety of affirming and inspiring components that instill a love for self, respect for culture, and expectation of achievement. Since children of color are often overlooked for participation in gifted and talented programs, a promising child of color that demonstrates high intellectual and academic abilities benefits greatly from a customized, diversified, individualized academic program that can only be created outside of an institution designed for the masses. In short, homeschooling is a legitimate, and often an essential option for gifted children of color to realize their highest potential.

Learning Differences & Disabilities

Learning differences are as varied and numerous as the humans themselves who possess them. However, there are a few overarching themes that categorize students into specific groups. These take on various names such as Auditory Processing Disorder, kinesthetic learner, Autism Spectrum Disorder, twice-exceptionality, Attention Deficit Disorder, Dyslexia, sensory processing disorder, the list goes on and on. Students in these groups often find themselves ill-served by traditional school because the nuances of their favored learning style cannot be individualized and incorporated into the curriculum. It is not uncommon for students with learning differences to have high IQs and to be intellectually gifted, but marginalized and diminished in traditional school settings. These students benefit from the individualized manipulation of resources to accommodate their learning style: in fact, research has found that students with ADHD are twice as academically engaged when homeschooled compared to those who undergo public schooling.

English Language Learners

The English Language Learners, formerly known as English as a Second Language (ESL) students, makeup roughly 10% of the students in America. In California, that percentage is over 20% and in Vermont it is 2%. While Spanish is the most common first language, the list it is estimated there are 800 different languages and dialects total in the world, a large majority of which are represented in classrooms today. Obviously, that adds an entirely new set of challenges. The trickiest issue with these learners is simply how diverse they are. The reason they are no longer referred to as "English Second Language" is because so many of them are actually learning English as a third, fourth, or fifth language. Translation proves complicated as there are variety of dialects and it can be harder than you might expect to find people fluent in English and the other language willing to work on documents. If you do manage to find one person, who will be their fact-checker, make sure they understand specific terms that are uncommon outside of education? Further, translation is really only one very small aspect. Idioms and sayings can be translated literally, and therefore will lose their meaning. Certain concepts and phrases only make sense from a certain cultural background. Teaching English to a student whose first language is Spanish isn't necessarily easy, but Spanish is very similar to English in many ways (same alphabet, very similar grammatical structure) whereas Mandarin, Russian, and Xhosa are worlds apart from English in a variety of ways.

ELL learners benefit from more visual styles of teaching and group work. ELL learners are also more likely to be quiet while they adapt to English, which can easily mask other factors like twice-exceptionality or giftedness. These students generally have parents who are not fluent in English, and thus are unable to utilize them as a resource for homework as many of their native classmates will, giving them yet another inherent disadvantage. More self-directed homeschooling could be beneficial while they acclimate to English, idioms, and cultural differences. Homeschooling can allow a tailored approach to incorporating learning English into their educational plan without compromising forward progress overall in academic performance and advancement. While non-English speaking homes will likely need support to ensure their homeschooled students become fluent in English, it is not a given that the school's ELL program will render more successful results. It's still important to get these kids out of the public system because they will need to learn English either way, but at home, they won't be performing poorly on the all-important tests simply because the tests were not designed with them in mind. ELLs are such a diverse group that it is nearly impossible on an inherent level for public schools to appropriately accommodate them.

College Success

Many might think that, after getting this far into the chapter, homeschooling has its benefits—but what happens when it is time to go to college? Will homeschool students be ready? The answer is yes, homeschoolers are ready for college and there are statistics that support this. The independence, engagement, and growth doesn't stop after graduation from homeschooling or at the end of summer break; as students who were homeschooled go on to college they still continue to succeed. Nearly 67% of homeschooled students graduate from college, compared to their "other school" counterparts, which includes public schools, who only attain a 57.5% graduation rate.

Homeschoolers not only thrive at home, they grow to be great students who know how they learn, study, and work best, an enviable skill set during the college years and beyond. If the student can understand themselves well enough to know what strategies and methods work best for them to learn, then they will more successfully adapt to the demands of post-secondary study than students who don't have that information.

So you have all these benefits with homeschooling, but one of the questions many have is: "I can't homeschool, so is it possible to go to college early, skip grades, and have more flexibility with what my student learns while they are in public school?"

Of course it is!

Consider for a moment how the K-12 years, and then college years, occur when our bodies and brains are forming and growing at amazing rates, which will never be equaled again. The challenges put upon our bodies and hormones are intense, and social pressures are at an all-time high. Couple that with the challenges of a flawed system and it is no wonder we have a drug crisis, mental illness epidemic, socially pervasive learning difficulties, and strained family relationships. To fit into this system is a big ask of our children. Homeschooling offers solutions to those challenges. If nothing else, it offers your student a voice in their life, a big ole' empowering voice, with flexibility and the knowledge that their parent is supporting them on that path less traveled.

References

Duvall, S. F., Delquadri, J. C., & Ward, D. L. (2004). A preliminary investigation into the effectiveness of homeschool instructional environments for students with Attention-Deficit/Hyperactivity Disorder. *School Psychology Review, 33*(1), 140–158. https://doi.org/10.1080/02796015.2004.12086238

Morris, E. W. & Perry, B. L. (2017). Girls behaving badly? Race, gender, and subjective evaluation in the discipline of African American girls. *American Sociological Association Sociology of Education, 90*(2), 127-148. https://doi.org/10.1177/0038040717694876

Taylor, M., & Schlitz, H. T. (2019). *The homeschool alternative: Incorporating a homeschool mindset for the benefit of black children in American.* Taylored Publishing.

Looking Back with Noel: Being the Only Girl

One of the worst things about being the "token" anything is feeling you represent your entire group. Throughout my childhood I was either the youngest, the only girl, or both. Being the youngest was awkward, but being the only girl was actively stressful at times because I thought whatever I did would reflect on all women and girls. I was good at math, but it wasn't that interesting to me so I didn't pursue it in my spare time, meaning the boys in my homeschool group surpassed me quickly. At the time I felt like an idiot because they all but told me so (or at least, it felt inferred), even though in retrospect all of us were wildly advanced regardless of whether some were more advanced than others. When you have one 8-year-old doing first-year college algebra, and another 8-year-old doing second-year college algebra, only the 8-year-olds notice the difference. For me, though, it felt like we were worlds apart. The truth is I was just as smart as the boys, smarter in some ways and slower in others, but because I was so thoroughly outnumbered, they were convinced that the ways I was smart were less important than their ways of being smart. As an adult with a doctorate in psychology, I find this attitude is still perpetuated at times, but I'm much more secure now than I was back then.

Being the only girl brought pain at times, pain that I usually hid, in the knowledge that it would be exploited if it were discovered. I learned that this can backfire when I was nine. I was on a robotics team with seven boys and I was the lone girl. Some of the boys were nicer than others, but none would exactly consider me a friend, at least not openly. We were divided into small groups to accomplish different tasks, and as a result, two other boys and I were in an area where no one else could really see us, although the others were just a few feet away. I finished my work early and the other two were still working, and being a bored nine-year-old girl I started goofing off, probably frolicking around or something but I don't remember for sure. They told me to stop because it was distracting and annoying. I told them, in some way or other, that they should've completed their work faster and that as the one who was done first, I would do whatever I wanted. One boy didn't like that much, so he grabbed a dry-erase marker and hit me on the head with it. I remember the edge of the bottom side hitting my scalp and resulting in a surprisingly sharp pain, but I lied outright and said: "that didn't hurt." Apparently, the other boy didn't appreciate that because he sucker-punched me in the stomach. Weirdly enough, I don't remember feeling that at all, I just remember keeling over instinctively without even really knowing what hit me. My memory is of being hurt emotionally more than physically, though I certainly felt both. I ran away crying and didn't tell anyone what happened, not out of a desire to hide what he did but more because I was confused and upset and too busy crying to make any sense (When younger kids start crying, their speech usually comes out as a jumble of whiny, whimper-y gibberish). The two moms in charge asked everyone what had happened, but I wasn't clear and the boys weren't honest.

I dried my tears, the day went on, and I ended up pretty chipper by the end of the day, by all accounts, because when my mom came to pick me up, I was just chatting away about all the robotics work we had completed. "Today was so fun! I worked on the coding to make the robot start the course! We were going to trigger it by waving a hand, but we realized that we accidentally waved the wrong way which triggered the robot to move backward, so we were really confused why it kept going backward until we figured that out. Then I was helping with the presentation we have to give to the judges about the robot..." Twenty minutes later, I suddenly decided it was worth mentioning that "the worst part of the day was when a boy hit me..."

Kudos to my mom for not flooring the brakes in shock in the middle of the highway during our hourlong drive home.

It is not over a decade later, and the boy who punched me is still a friend and still feels really bad about hitting me. The boy who hit me with the marker is still not a friend and I'd guess he still doesn't feel bad about hitting me.

As time goes by, I see more and more support for women's issues in the gifted community. My biggest issue is that we're still so focused on "women in STEM" and yet we don't see the value of actually appreciating the fields women already dominate. If you include nursing and psychology in STEM (which you should, based on the definition of science), the gap isn't so bad. Trust me, I still want there to be more balance in computer science and the like, but if the only way we can measure a woman's contribution to society against the contributions of men, then we're just adopting a different type of sexism rather than truly providing a solution to it.

Homeschooling was an invaluable resource as a girl. In traditional schooling, girls are called on less, their ideas are often dismissed, and they are bullied by both male and female classmates. For a history on this, see Zimmerman and West's *Sex roles, Interruptions, and Silences in Conversation*, or Corrine Monnet's *Gender Roles in Conversation*. There is also Sadker & Sadker's more recent *Failing at Fairness: How America's Schools Cheat Girls*. Homeschooling doesn't fix sexism or anything, but it offers an incredible advantage: online programs mean that students can choose the anonymity of a name rather than a face, decreasing the opportunity for bias; one-on-one teaching with a parent (which only represents one piece of the homeschooling puzzle, but it is still a valuable tool) cannot be biased or sexist since there is no dismissing or ignoring in a class of one; and lastly, parents have more control and support to observe and intervene when bullying or exclusion is taking place. Sure, you probably shouldn't step in and fix every problem that your child encounters, but the opportunity for stronger supervision is still entirely worth it.

I have a few final thoughts on this subject. For "only girls," I have a few pieces of advice: don't let outside perception affect the way you see yourself or your personality; don't be afraid of being too feminine or too masculine and instead just try to be genuine. However, my biggest call to action is not to the girls but to the parents, educators, and facilitators. Take sexism seriously. Kids tend to live in strongly gender-segregated worlds and it *is* avoidable. We don't have to let them treat each other like garbage, especially for reasons as arbitrary and harmful as gender. You can't always intervene for many reasons, and frankly, you shouldn't always intervene, but stand up for your kids, and perhaps more importantly, correct them when they're wrong.

Looking Back with Haley: What's the Hurry?

Sixteen is an interesting number in our society. For a girl, it is perceived as "sweet" and a rite of passage to becoming a woman. In many ways sixteen can define who you think you are and what you can be. I am very aware of this paradox because I am sixteen years old.

Think back to your junior year of high school. What was life like? What was important and popular? Did you know what your life purpose would be? *Did you ever think, I wish I could just get on with life?*

My parents didn't have all the answers, but the one thing they knew for sure was this: In life, the only constant is change.

I started my education as a child in private schools largely to accommodate my parent's need for extended day-care hours as they both worked long hours. When we moved to Texas, I started at public school where I remained through fifth grade. After fifth grade, my mother pulled me out of public school. I was ten years old.

I graduated from high school three years later at the age of thirteen and started community college. I did a year at community college (including summers, and mini-semesters to rack up core credits) and then transferred to TWU when I was fourteen as a junior. I spent two years at TWU and graduated at the age of sixteen Magna Cum Laude with nine law school acceptance letters with scholarships.

When parents hear my story they often ask: "How did you go from a publicly schooled ten-year-old fifth-grader to a high-school graduate and college freshman in three years?" Usually, they are asking because they realize that traditional school may not be working as well as expected for their own ten-year-old, and knowing I started my accelerated journey so "late" is motivation for them to consider it for their child.

When my parents first removed me from public school, they were totally new to homeschooling. My father was skeptical, but my mother was optimistic. For two years, they opted to enroll me in what is known as a "hybrid school." A hybrid school is a part-time brick-and-mortar school that offers classes to homeschooled students twice a week. This allows the student to get their lesson plans and instruction from hired teachers in a classroom setting. Then, they come home and work their syllabus for the rest of the time at home. Parents have total control over what their student learns, and how they learn it with the ability to opt out of any assignment (or add enrichment). Grades are provided, but the grades that are given by the teacher are only one component of the overall grade in the class. The parent uses the teacher feedback, and whatever other assessment tools they choose, to report a final grade for their student on the student's transcript.

With no mandated state testing, the curriculum can be diverse, tailored, and relevant to the student meeting specific aims based on their future desires and their natural talents. However, teachers do periodically perform learning assessments that are private and used by the parents to help direct their child's learning. There are also opportunities for students to take standardized exams. For instance, my mother signed me up to take the ACT for the seventh-grade talent search when I was twelve. I retook the ACT for university applications when I was thirteen (it was a requirement for some of the colleges and universities I considered transferring to). I also took the SAT because my mother wanted to compare my scores on both exams "for fun." I took and passed the CLEP in college algebra for core college math credit when I was thirteen. I also took the TSI (Texas Success Initiative) and the Accuplacer for placement on college classes at the community college level. I was also a competitive "mathlete" and took the AMC (American Math Competition) exams and the USMTS (US Mathematical Talent Search). Although I was homeschooled, I took lots of standardized exams so we could ascertain my readiness for college, gain college credit, practice test preparation, but my academic program was never centered around the test.

After being at the hybrid school for two years, I was ready for more advanced math than could be easily provided in that setting. My mother correctly assumed that I didn't like math because of the way it was taught in public school. Once in the hybrid school, I was able to really explore math and learn at my own pace. I quickly went through pre-algebra, algebra, geometry, and intermediate algebra during those years at the hybrid school. Once we got to pre-calculus, my mother looked to the community college with the intention of having me take that one class there. However, after passing the TSI and placing into pre-calculus, she decided to explore this option more deeply. This is how I ended up at the community college at age thirteen.

When I applied to four-year colleges and universities as a transfer, I was accepted into every single one of the seventeen colleges I applied to. These schools ranged from HBCUs

(Historically Black Colleges and Universities) such as Xavier University of Louisiana's Biomedical Scholar Honors Program to Spelman College and Tuskegee University. I was accepted into private schools such as University of Dallas and Bard at Simon's Rock, as well as local state public schools such at University of Texas at Dallas and Texas Woman's University. After much deliberation, I chose TWU for my undergraduate education because as a 13-year-old young woman, I felt safe on a campus of (almost) all women. And the diversity of the student body and faculty was a key factor because I didn't want to have to fight for recognition as a young Black woman. It was an excellent choice for me. My giftedness was appreciated and uniqueness celebrated. The Dean even created a new degree plan for me because I was going to be too young to sit for the TExES exam, so I completed an educational leadership degree that allowed me to focus more on special populations of students and educational equity advocacy.

Finally, I am often asked: "What's the rush? Why don't you take a gap year?"

One thing that bugs me is when people act like taking one year off when you're 18 years old is enough time to "find yourself" or will otherwise offer some great insight into your future plans. You can't know what you want to do without exposure to information about the options. College offers that. Therefore, if you are unclear about your future plans, it actually makes more sense to go to college and not take a "gap year." As you "find yourself," you could be checking off boxes on those core classes at community college, easily and inexpensively online. Then, after a couple of years, when those core classes are done, transferring to a four-year college or university that accepts the bulk (or all) of those credits means you'll get a degree for half the price, less stress, and without significant sacrifice of time or energy, leaving you more time to explore other life options and opportunities (especially if you are very young and would be in compulsory school anyway). I knew that anything I wanted to do with my life would require at *least* a college degree. I was also aware of the fact that I would not regret getting a degree (even if I never used or needed it), but I might regret not having it one day. Black women need credentials if their voices are to be heard and their contributions valued in the workforce (and even with credentials we are systematically disrespected). It was never an option for me to forego a college education. Why not realize my full potential? Why delay it?

Further, I am not going through school to "get a job." Rather, I am learning and acquiring my education and the necessary credentials to start living my life *outside* of the confines of formal educational environments. So many young people yearn to live their lives outside of "school" and feel college only hinders that (and it does). How awesome would it be to get a college degree by age eighteen when most people are just getting a high-school diploma? Now, the decision to attend college is a non-issue. All the narratives about the cons of college and higher education are mitigated if the student has a bachelor's degree by age seventeen or eighteen. I believe the same can be said about an advanced degree in an area such as law, or a Ph.D.

What's the hurry? The hurry is that I don't want to be in school forever. I have dreams and aspirations that extend beyond formal education and classrooms. I want to live in the world and get out there and find my way. But I understand that an education and credentials are key elements to my success—especially as a woman of color. Therefore, I am eager to flit through these pages so I can move on to the next chapter.

My journey to my version of sixteen started when I was just eleven years old. It was at this point in time I realized that in order to discover and create my life's purpose, I had to move beyond the path general education had been paved for me. I had to move past high school. Realizing that most of high-school was a repeat or extension of middle-school motivated me to prove to that I deserved to be in college. I had to find a path that allowed me to pursue the "me" that I wanted to be. Homeschooling allowed me such an avenue: to take my own path and demonstrate my ability.

Motivated by these challenges, I graduated from my homeschool high-school and started college at the age of thirteen. I understand that the only way to know your limits is to test them. To be great and realize our full potential as human beings on this earth, we cannot be afraid to be bold, and to fail. Being bold entails deviating from the paved road and having the courage to trail blaze new ones.

Chapter 8
Improving Your Education without Homeschooling

Homeschooling isn't just a practice, it's also a mindset: the acceptance that public education is unlikely to cover everything your student needs. Parental involvement is an integral part of the success of almost all students. You don't have to homeschool in order to supplement your student's education, to skip grades, or even to go to college early. Yet, a homeschool mindset helps you consider a broader spectrum of educational choices and long-term goals.

When you start expanding your mindset about education, you realize how much your student could be doing to become a stronger college candidate, a more focused learner, and quite frankly, open their world to more interesting experiences. The things you sign them up for and how you guide them through school will drastically be impacted by your approach to education.

What does your student enjoy doing? How can an extracurricular activity help expand or grow those interests? Thinking this way really puts your mindset to the test, are you signing your student up for this activity because it will look good on a resume? Is it a passion? Or is it just because you did it as a child? Are you signing them up because all of the other parents did? These are all good questions to ask that a public school mindset rarely evokes. Often, parents will sign their student up for an activity because the student wants to be with their friends/that's what all the other parents are doing. A homeschool mindset has a slightly broader and more profound approach.

The homeschool mindset means paying special attention to the environment of any activity involving your student. Obviously, you want to avoid any toxic environments. But think deeper about choices your student makes. Are they in clubs that allow hazing, unhealthy competition, or unfair treatment? Or is it an environment that promotes teamwork and celebrating the achievements of others? A public school mindset often means thinking "that's good that my student is getting involved on campus" or "I am glad that my student gets to have a good time with their friends," and both of these are valid considerations, but we encourage deeper consideration. When considering the purpose of signing them up in the first place, it is helpful to check yourself and any baggage you, as a parent, bring to the equation. What you did as a child, what you enjoyed as you were growing up, or your experiences in particular activities are valid, but should not overwhelm the student's own personality and desires.

The homeschool mindset is especially important if you wish to subject accelerate or skip grades. Public school tends to discourage acceleration, as will anyone who listens to opinion rather than evidence. Fortunately, you can skip ahead in terms of content even if at school you are not in a position to skip full grades, whether that be because of academic readiness or institutional opposition. Exposing your child to higher-level homework in math, science, or any other subject when they get home can help them stay motivated in topics of interest. It is easy for students to get into the habit of only thinking about "what they need for the test" but that mindset does not promote creativity or cultivate passions.

If you have a student who is working in a grade lower than their intellectual abilities, they can quickly get bored and do poorly on exams and in class. Many parents assume that if a student has poor grades, it is because they are not applying themselves. They would be correct, but not necessarily because the student isn't capable of achieving. It seems counterintuitive that easy material would result in poor grades, but work that is tedious or lacking in challenge absolutely can.

No matter your child's curriculum needs or your schedule, a broader perspective on education can easily be integrated into your daily life. Homeschooling has many benefits that the public school system cannot provide; equally, there are ways to work with your public school education to provide your students with better options. Subject acceleration is possible when a student can show mastery of a class and needs more rigorous coursework. That can be demonstrated in numerous ways, including credit by examination, departmental recommendation, or simply taking the public school class during summer or night school.

The library and the Internet can be the great equalizers in terms of access to self-directed learning. Kids can teach themselves to code, learn higher level math concepts, or dive into almost anything. Some colleges, including MIT, provide courses for free. Khan Academy covers a multitude of topics. TED talks cover just about everything under the sun and outside our galaxy.

Something as simple as having your child write three papers or give you three presentations on topics of interest (or topics they know nothing about) will expand their worldview and brush up on ideas and concepts they may want to explore. The possibilities are limitless. Younger kids can research gerbils, or Disney movies, or the history of action toys. Older kids can learn about the history of race car driving or compare the engines of yesteryear to today; they can learn how to write an "app" or why mosquitoes are the most dangerous life form on earth. How about inspiring a budding artist or entomologist by tracing pictures of insects and coloring them in with the opposite colors from the color wheel. Writing a song with the same chord structure as a Beatles' tune or giving a presentation or performance of the most famous operas. A power point slide show of the most famous art pieces in the known world would be great for the whole family. The universe is a fascinating place—helping a kid to find a passion, or a niche, or if nothing else a "fun fact" they can share with others is a worthy endeavor.

Scouting, churches, and other non-profits offer opportunities to volunteer and gain leadership experience. Passions are often born from experiences. Most kids don't know what they want to be when they "grow up"—we have to provide experiences to help them learn about their options. We have to provide opportunities to stretch their imagination and conversely also have them understand the reality of some dreams. It's safe to say that most medical doctors didn't fumble and stumble their way into medical school, internships, residencies, passing their licensing exam, and then just being a great doctor. There is a vision, a plan, and hard work. On the same note, the notion of an "overnight sensation" musician/actor/etc. is often inaccurate: those artists have had to work on their craft with a passion. As Louis Pasteur said, "Fortune favors the prepared mind."

From sleepaway to day camps, summer offers an embarrassment of riches when it comes to opportunities for all ages. Organizations and colleges offer classes for credit and enrichment. There are academic camps all over the country, as well as community colleges offering programs locally. Recreation centers, zoos, enrichment schools, etc. offer opportunities for students, as well. Summer is also a perfect time to hire a college student to tutor/teach a topic of interest to your children. A biology or physics major could demonstrate some fascinating experiments and discuss their passions for the joy of it, with no need for grades. An English major could help hone some writing or literary analysis skills. Learning a foreign language could happen through immersion camps or local teachers.

Finding opportunities to feed the heart, soul, and mind, is not generally easy. Perhaps your public school does a good job of that, if so, count yourself fortunate. If not, using Internet search engines, social media, and networking is the next step. There are Yahoo groups, Facebook pages, webpages, ad nauseam. There's no Yellow Pages for education where you can "let your fingers do the walking", but your fingers can definitely do the typing and search for information about space camps, math camps, writing camps, etc. Just to get you started, here are a few places to start:

- MathCounts
- Duke TIP (Talent Identification Program)
- Jack Kent Cooke scholarship
- Caroline D. Bradley Scholarship
- Northwestern Center for Talent Development
- Johns Hopkins Center for Talented Youth

Public and private school advocacy is a lesson in persistence and patience. The challenges generally include bureaucracy, tradition, and the fear of opening the floodgates. Leadership tends to want to stick with the status quo as it makes things easier for them. Knowing your rights, not accepting the first "no" you hear, and documenting your journey in whatever you are trying to accomplish is a good start. Remember, no one knows your child as well as you do. Advocating for their academic needs to be met is not pushy or demanding, it is a reasonable expectation.

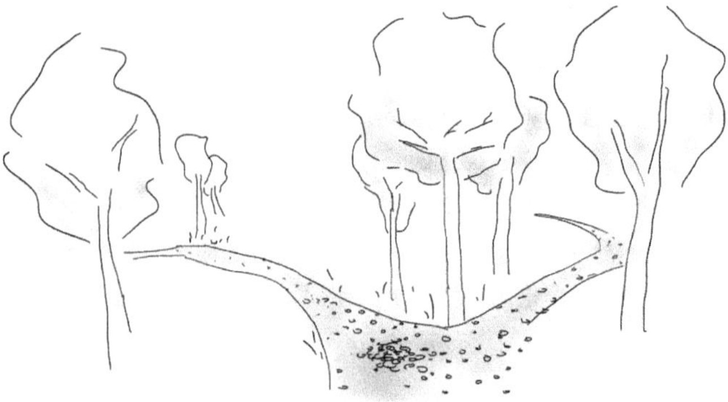

Looking Back with Nancy: Try Something Different

As the years passed, we considered other educational options. Not that we were unhappy with homeschooling; we just wanted to stay open to new possibilities. At ages 10 and 11, Noel tested for admission into the Davidson Academy in Reno, Nevada. It is the only public middle/high school for the Profoundly Gifted in the U.S.A. It is free but requires certain test scores to apply, and a lengthy application before being considered for a placement test. We were willing to move for this opportunity. The placement test is an all-day experience of being a part of the school and its students. She loved it. However, she was not offered admission. She tested again the next year. Rejected. She was not willing to try a third time. In hindsight, she was thankful that she took the path she did. But at the time, it hurt a lot. We were surprised at the time, but we learned that even amazing schools will not be a fit for everyone.

Her ego was certainly bruised from that first rejection and imposter syndrome started to kick in. "Imposter syndrome" causes gifted kids and adults to feel their intelligence is somehow fraudulent, despite overwhelming evidence to the contrary. Noel was especially good at logic. She loved logic puzzles and critical thinking exercises. At age 10, we paid what was big bucks for us, $400, for her to take a college-level online class in Propositional Calculus, aka Logic. It was hard. I was unable to help beyond the introduction pages. Luckily there was a professor available by email, offering the occasional telephone call. She worked hard at this class and earned an A+. It was a huge deal for her. Mom grades and Mom's friends' grades and kudos are nice and all, but earning every point to score 95% in a college-level class is certainly helpful to a young ego. You would not think she needed this, but she did. So, as it goes, one door closes and a window opens.

Probably the most amazing door that opened for us was finding a brilliant, beautiful, passionate, female mathematician that tutored smart kids. Noel was her first female student. Alicia was studying for her Ph.D. She made Noel work, she made her cry, and she left a life-long impression. She taught her so much about math but was also an amazing counsel about boys in those pre-teen years, college life as a young teen, and as an older teen during her Ph.D. program. She was also Noel's "Plus One" for her stint on the first "Who Wants To Be A Millionaire—Whiz Kids Week."

When Noel was 11, Alicia allowed Noel to attend the College Algebra class she was teaching at a local university. Most of the material was a repeat of what she already knew, but some was new. Noel was Alicia's go-to student for solving the problems on the chalkboard if no one else would volunteer. There was a deaf student in that class and the University provided an ASL interpreter. Noel found that fascinating and can still remember how to sign "the function of X." Noel didn't always find it easy to concentrate on the lecture with this distraction. It was also a summer class which meant longer lecture times. So, was she a perfect student with perfect grades? Nope. Was that okay? Yep.

At age 12, with the Davidson Academy now off the table, the stars aligned as we came to consider entry into an IB school, a private Christian school, and a brand-new early college STEM high school. We researched all of these options, we went to open houses, we met with people, we pondered, we prayed. When we were almost done, Noel said she wanted to stick with homeschooling. But I insisted we finish the search process. We went to one more event for the early college STEM high school. She changed her mind. She wanted to start 9th grade as a 7th grader age-wise and attend this school. That two-year jump actually represented a serious regression for her academically, but we thought the unique opportunities this school would offer would offset this step backward academically. She was required to take Credit by Examination (CBE) tests. Over the course of a couple of weeks, she sat for six different exams each of which lasted three hours each. Easy peasy. She was now a 12-year-old high school student with the babyface and braces to go with it.

The long and short of her one semester of public high school was that it was not a good fit. Despite dedicated administrators and teachers, academically it was an often slow repeat of material she long since knew. Socially, although some kids were nice enough, most were not. It was the school's first year, there were still kinks to be worked out, and, sadly, too many students who did not really want to be there. The disrespect towards teachers and the off-campus activities of some students were overwhelming for Noel. Her sense of empathy left her worried about kids coming from less-than-ideal homes and those lacking motivation to improve their situations. And that weight was heavy. We guessed wrong, we should have stuck to homeschooling.

Yet, as that door closed, the experience of this high school and its relationship with the local community college opened the window for early college options. She sat for the tests the college required just a few weeks after turning thirteen. After officially completing one semester of public high school, she started her first real college classes soon thereafter. Though the hope of a more typical high school experience was quickly dashed, the challenge and excitement of college at thirteen was a fantastic replacement.

The old saying of when a door closes a window opens is a positive affirmation that there is more than one way to get from point A to point B. When you have to navigate education off the beaten path, many doors get closed, but guess what—there are other doors and several windows out there also. Trying something different can be scary and exhilarating. Showing respectful diligence to advocate for your child is a powerful weapon in the parenting toolbox. Modeling perseverance and adaptability is the best way to teach it. Power on!

Looking Back with Myiesha: Our Community College Path to Early College

There were many reasons we chose community college for our daughter, and after completing her first community college class with an A, we feel pretty good about this decision. The first reason for this choice is that our local community college is close to our home, it's a safe school, and our son was on the swim team there so she had already had plenty of exposure to the campus. The second reason is best encapsulated in the phrase "big fish, little pond." I am an advocate of being in an academic environment that challenges the student but also allows their (individual) achievements to be recognized.

In his book, *David and Goliath*, Malcolm Gladwell makes the point that being a big fish in a small pond is often beneficial and quite possibly the defining feature of post-graduate success in competitive scientific fields. The point is made that an average student at an elite Ivy League school is likely a top tier student at a local State school. However, because of their environment, students of similar caliber often have mixed success at post-graduate level due to the fact that those "big fish" have a stronger sense of self-esteem than those same students in environments where they are perceived as "below average." Therefore, being at a local or state school can do wonders for the self-esteem and ultimately have better academic outcomes for some of the most competitive students.

It is also worth noting that Texas community colleges and public universities share a common credit system. If the courses taken at the community college have a common number, the credit is accepted. This means that you lose no credit (or time) when making the transfer.

However, there are specific transfer points after the first year and second year. I plotted out the practical difference for Haley with tentative course-work. The first option was to transfer after two years—our original plan. The advantage of this was that Haley would then be 16. Transfer to a "far away" university became an option at this age, depending on various factors, if she had an associate's degree and the ability to manage her affairs.

However, transfer after *two* years creates a situation where many second-year courses may not be accepted as major credit. And that is almost guaranteed if the transfer school is prestigious, which was ultimately the only reason to leave home. Therefore, a year is added to the program. The alternative is to transfer after one year with 30 credits. This is advantageous over transferring with less than 30 units because no high-school credentials are necessary once you acquire 30+ units. No SAT/ACT, no AP, and no high-school GPA. Ridding herself of these hoops were very attractive to Haley. As a homeschooled student, it is helpful to not have to "justify" your transcript, or otherwise "prove" competency (beyond the TSI, and the ACT she already took).

In Texas, Community College is like a secret back-door into college without all the "high-school drama." Haley literally "skipped" conventional high-school and completed her schooling in a dually enrolled environment, earning college credit. The most important factor for Haley was the immediacy: No waiting, no age-restrictions in applying to and attending community college.

In listening to *my* kid, and *her* thoughts, I had to make some adjustments to my original plan. Recall, my original plan had her going to Harvard, so she had to jump thru all of the hoops. But when your plans involve somebody else's life, you have to be open to constant recalibration. So, instead of going the traditional (homeschool entry) route, I decided to have her do dual-enrollment (DE) class. After one DE course, I felt comfortable allowing her to go full-time to community college.

I started keeping a high-school transcript in middle-school since kids may be doing high-school level stuff before "high-school age," and they should get credit for that. Therefore, she had *way* more than the necessary credits to graduate—which in Texas is only 22 (especially since I incorporated credit for leadership into her transcript, gained via Jack and Jill). I also included credit for community service—gained via Rhoer Club of Sigma Gamma Rho Sorority. I also gave her music credit from her private lessons and elective credit from orchestra. She worked at weddings as a harpist, so I had her run that like a business (meeting with brides, establishing musical repertoire, attire, etc.) and gave her credit for that: "Introduction to Entrepreneurship."

By the time she was 12, she had *plenty* credits that were viable to put on a transcript for high-school credit. Additionally, we worked year-round on the core subjects of Math and Language Arts.

For us, it made total sense to go ahead and graduate her from homeschool high-school so she could get the number of necessary credits to be eligible to transfer to University. Here in Texas, UT Dallas will automatically accept a transfer with 42+ credits (which was initially our/my target school). So, the sooner the student can engage in the community college system and get those credits the sooner they can move on.

Part 3
Early College

Early college is the topic the four of us are asked to speak on the most, and yet, one that is often so difficult to describe. The biggest obstacle to early college is simply that people don't even think to consider it. "I didn't realize you could apply before 18." "I just assumed that I had to ask permission before enrolling my 10-year-old kid at community college." "You obviously need to graduate high school before going to college, right? And you can't graduate high school until 18!"

As you'll learn soon enough, early college is actually much easier, much simpler, and much less stressful than it sounds at first. One theme of this book so far has been thinking outside the box. You probably hear that phrase a lot, to the point that it can lose its meaning at times, but it is important that you understand what this really entails. There are constraints that we never think to question until we do. We are in an era where the rules, roles, and expectations of yesteryear are losing their influence. Though it brings controversy, it brings new opportunities and new avenues of exploration. As so many sectors of existence seem to be undergoing revolutions of their own, let us hope that the much-overdue educational revolution is on the horizon.

Chapter 9
Starting Early College

Possibly the biggest question about early college is the most basic one: How?! As in, how is it feasible logistically to enter college early? There is a long answer, but the short one is that it's much easier than you think. Let's start off by establishing some information you may not be aware of:

1. You do **not** need a high school diploma to be accepted to every college.
2. Homeschool **is** an acceptable method to attain a high school diploma.
3. You do **not** need to be any specific age to apply to college, and they are unlikely to ask about your age unless **you** bring it up.
4. You do **not** need to ask for permission to attend college under the age of 18.
5. If you want to earn your diploma first, you will have to skip grades to enter college. This can be done inside or outside of traditional schooling. If you don't want to earn your diploma, you'll have to stand out to get accepted.
6. The savings associated with living at home and/or attending community college for part of the college experience are significant, and barring significant scholarship awards, state schools are more economical than private schools. We hate to be the bearer of bad news, but financial aid rarely meets all the students' needs.

When parents take control of their child's education, a major concern is college-readiness. According to ACT, only 38% of students who took the ACT in 2018 met college readiness benchmarks in the four core subject areas. And this percentage is lower than in years past. Assuming public school will prepare students for college is unwise: therefore, a plan of action to prepare a child for college is essential to maintain future career options.

Application process

When conducting business online, including college applications, standardized exam registration, scholarship applications, and more, the Children's Online Privacy Protection Act of 1998 (COPPA) limits a parent's ability to use online resources. As such, creating a FAFSA, registering for SAT, ACT, or CLEP, even making a college application can have unforeseen obstacles regarding online registration and use if your student is under the age of 13. Therefore, additional time should be set aside for paper copy registration for students under the age of 13 in these circumstances.

Applications to college for the young student are otherwise identical to any other student. Many colleges use the Common Application or some other computerized application. Community colleges are a great starting point for many young students because of their convenience, the option to select multiple courses, the online options, the low cost, and their high accessibility. Community colleges will have either a placement exam, such as the Accuplacer, or allow submission of standardized test scores to show college-readiness.

There are also dual-enrollment (DE) options for young students who want to start college early. There may be rules and regulations regarding what grade makes a child eligible to consider this option, and there is often a limit on the number and types of courses that can be taken for DE. This option is fantastic because it brings credibility to a homeschool transcript by demonstrating to colleges and universities the student's ability to do college coursework in a college setting. Most core classes can be satisfied with this option. The drawbacks are the restrictions that may be placed on some younger students, as discussed earlier.

Creating a homeschool transcript for your homeschool student allows you to award credits for life experience, for exams, and allow graduation once high-school requirements have been met. Graduation from homeschool high-school allows the student to enroll full-time in a community college and also take advantage of student services on campus—such as tutoring, and study groups. It also eliminates the dual-enrollment restriction. Therefore, the student can take any of the classes offered, as well as the number of classes desired.

Preparation for college and ascertaining college readiness

There are various ways to ascertain college readiness ranging from objective standardized testing to dual-enrollment course-work achievement. Standardized exams such as the SAT (Scholastic Aptitude Test) and the ACT (American College Test) are two of the most popular options and are universally accepted by all colleges and universities in the United States. A high enough score on these exams demonstrates academic college-readiness to higher education institutions which can prove valuable for students who are seeking non-traditional paths into college due to its more objective nature.

If a child is advanced in a single subject, taking a CLEP (College Level Exam Program) exam is a great way to demonstrate a degree of knowledge at college-level in that area. This can be a valuable tool in helping students engage in specific college coursework even if they are not academically ready across the board. It is also affordable and can be retaken in six months if the score is not acceptable. College websites will tell you what CLEPs they accept. Whether or not the said score is accepted at the university the child eventually attends, it is still an excellent means of proving mastery in a specific area.

The Accuplacer is an exam that also assesses college-readiness and areas where some remediation will be necessary; it also provides a wealth of information to help steer educational foci and allows the student to test into appropriate college course levels. When a student demonstrates college-readiness using an objective measure, advocating for their inclusion in college classrooms is more effective.

The Accuplacer is administered by the College Board and students typically make an appointment to take the exam by contacting their local college advising office. The exam is not timed and evaluates college-readiness in the areas of math, reading, and writing.

There are also more subjective measures of college readiness, which are more nuanced and difficult to ascertain. The skills necessary to successfully navigate an in-person college course include having the ability to be still and listen, take notes, and participate in discussions by asking questions and engaging the professor and fellow students. The young college student must be trustworthy and have an adult advocate who will oversee the process, assess safety, and provide supervision when necessary. The student must be able to regulate his or her emotions and follow instructions. It is certainly helpful if the child is easy to coach and can take direction.

Some colleges and universities may allow a young student to audit a class (as described in Nancy's story in the previous chapter) which allows for enrichment, self-exploration, and academic enhancement without the stress of worrying about a grade. Auditing a class means taking a class without the benefits or drawbacks of grades, and no college credit will be earned. This may be a great option for some students to ascertain college-readiness without risking the possibility of a low grade and sabotaging the college-level Grade Point Average.

A drawback of auditing a class is frequently registration for auditors follows students taking it for credit which may leave an auditor with less desirable instructors or class times. (It is not possible to audit over-registered classes.) Further, there is the drawback in terms of time and money spent which will ultimately lead to no college credit being accrued; thus, effort and financial investment are not maximized.

Cost

Early college usually means living at home, and that means saving money. Dorm rent and meal plans are not cheap! Colleges sometimes require that freshmen live on campus, but waivers are given for a variety of reasons, so rarely is one "forced" to live in a dorm. Living at home is not a requirement for early college, of course, and it depends on what will work best for the student. Many early college students may find that they save significant amounts of money if they stay at home. Some worry that this trade-off will mean loss of scholarships, but again, that depends on the grade performance so far, as well as the overall interest in relying on academic scholarships.

How to document high-school for the homeschooled student

Creating a high-school transcript is essential. On that transcript, the parent can award credit for material learned at home or homeschool classes, life-experience, credit by exam, dual-enrollment credit, and even courses taken online, as well as public or private schools. The total sum of all the students' academic accomplishments must be represented in the transcript. This notarized transcript is universally accepted at all colleges and universities in America.

There are many online guidelines and forums to help craft a transcript, and some schools have specific requests on what should be documented on the transcript. Knowing this ahead of time will help ensure you fulfill requirements. Additionally, a high-school diploma can be ordered from organizations such as the HSLDA (Homeschool Legal Defense Association). There are online communities that also provide transcript and diploma replicas. However, the most important documentation is actually the transcript itself.

In summary, the steps to getting into college early require the same documents and completion of the same tasks as getting into college at any age. Depending on the specific requirements of the college or university, the SAT or ACT may be required. For homeschool students, some universities require SAT subject tests. Dual enrollment that takes place on an actual college campus (vs at a local high-school) can add tremendous value in legitimizing a homeschool transcript. CLEP and AP exams (both of which can be taken by homeschool students) can add value by demonstrating to college admission officers the academic readiness of a young student for university-level study. Ascertaining college readiness on a social and emotional level is also as essential as academic readiness. Documenting the activities, progress, and course of study on a transcript is equally essential—colleges will ask for a transcript, not a high-school diploma.

Applying for college is a stressful process, no matter how you do it. Determining exactly when a student is ready is subjective. K-12 public school doesn't guarantee such readiness or maturity. What any particular college desires of its applicants is also fairly fluid. There was a time when colleges required a multitude of standardized test scores. Some colleges now are doing away with even requiring an SAT or ACT, much less a plethora of AP tests and SAT Subject Tests. The cost of attendance as well as the rising student debt are serious considerations. Less informed parents and students assume their cost will be minimal because of scholarships. There just aren't enough to go around for all the deserving students. And while any scholarship is beneficial, a $1000 scholarship does not go far when you factor in tuition, fees, books, room, and board, etc. Having the documentation and credentials a homeschooler might need is not so overwhelming as long as you keep good records. As we said before, we put a man on the moon with less technology than your smart phone, and a few internet searches and college websites should provide you with enough information. Obviously, early college isn't right for everyone—and it has its risks of road bumps—but it is worth a conversation with everyone.

Looking Back with Nancy: Early College (or, a Plexiglas Door as a Metaphor *for* Parent-Adolescent Dynamics)

Community college was a wonderful place for a 13-year-old with acne, braces, and an overwhelming desire to learn. Although a few students were a bit surprised and confused by Noel's age, they were generally too busy with their adult lives and their grades to care much about other students. Bullying and high school drama were nowhere to be seen. Joining a few clubs provided some camaraderie, intellectual dialogue, and fun, although the main goal was to learn. Learn the material, learn to be organized, learn how to study, learn how to take notes, learn how to talk to adults, etc. No need to learn how to be a popular kid, to find the cool crowd, or deal with that all-important question of high school: where to sit for lunch. That was not an issue at our local community college. The age range of students and their motivations were wide-ranging—plenty wide to allow for a younger student.

Noel started off with two compressed classes in March of 2012. At first, I walked her to class and sat nearby. It was a bonus when the professor left the door open so I could hear and enjoy learning too. I never interacted with any professor until the end of the semester. I wish I could have photographed the startled and confused expressions we saw when she introduced me to her professors as her mom, she announced she was 13, told them they had permission to talk with me privately, and then walked away. They obviously all recognized she was young, but they had assumed she was no younger than 16, as the official rules at the time were that dual-enrollment was only available to high school juniors and seniors. All I really wanted to know was whether she contributed appropriately to class discussions and had been respectful to the professor and her classmates. If she had been too shy to talk, or too obnoxious to be considerate, those would have been issues to address. Maturity can only really be proven through experience. I helped her set up her web portal, and this meant I knew her grades and could help her stay organized; intellect and executive functioning skills do not always go hand-in-hand, perhaps even through adulthood. They certainly didn't for my 13-year old: reminders were given here and there, and I enjoyed proofreading her emails and assignments...not just for grammar errors, but also for sass (which is Noel's first language).

The local community college option was an affordable and less stressful choice than a university would have been. The well-qualified and passionate professors were just the icing on the cake. We were and remain thankful.

Our original plan was for Noel to stay at Tarrant County College for three or four years and make that her "high school experience." Our decision to leave community college came rather suddenly after attending Phi Theta Kappa's (community college honor society) College Night, as well as a homeschool college night on the same evening in late January of 2013. We both left thinking the exact same thing: that even though she had just turned 14, she was ready for more. So, we made the impulsive decision to see if we could get her into a university *that fall*. More reasoned people would have thought longer and harder about this change in the long term plan. For better or worse, Noel and I both skewed a bit more toward intuition and quick thinking vs. pondering and plodding along logically.

To justify this decision, I felt she needed to prove herself as a full-time student vs. the part-time, dual-enrolled student she was at the time. She was only taking 11 hours, but my gut told me she needed to succeed as a full-time student before she went off to a university. Yet, to enroll her full-time at the community college, I had to officially graduate her from our homeschool high school. That decision would take away her freshman status and potentially more scholarship money. You can't make an omelet without breaking some eggs, so we changed her status, added more classes, and began the college application process as a transfer admission.

The intention was to stay in the Dallas/Fort Worth metroplex to earn her undergraduate degree. She wanted to keep up with her friends, church, all-girl rock band, Girl Scout troop, etc. So we quickly applied to three local schools we thought might be a good fit. Again, more reasoned people perhaps would have applied to more. As we were in the process of doing this, I became convinced she should apply to Texas A&M. It is arguably the best public university in the state and we were familiar with it via various outreach opportunities that the Math, Physics, and Engineering departments had done with our state group for profoundly gifted children. I also had a gut feeling. Call it what you want: intuition, a sign from God, a message from the universe, or just personal bias. Whatever it was, all I can say is that it was screaming "apply to A&M!" Noel was reluctant as she didn't see herself leaving DFW, but she trusted me. More admission essays were written and another application fee was paid.

Since we were putting the cart before the horse, as it were, she applied before we did campus tours. We scrambled to get those done. It was a busy spring. She was promptly offered admission to the three schools she initially applied to. She had applied to Texas A&M last, so we waited to see if she would be admitted. We scheduled for her to sit in on classes as best we could: not every school allows for that. We talked to admissions and financial aid. She talked to professors and department heads. When all was said and done and for a myriad of reasons, she did not want to attend any of the three schools to which she had been accepted. As we left one of those universities, heavy-hearted that what had once been seen as three good choices was now three mediocre options, we returned home dejected only to check her email to see her admission to Texas A&M had come through that very same day! God is good!

So, in late April of 2013, we quickly pivoted to the idea of the two of us living in a cheap apartment close to school and her joining more than 55,000 students on the sprawling campus in College Station: three hours from DFW. We never considered her living on campus. We knew she was too young and we/she were not ready for her to live on her own.

It was an exciting time! I was so thankful that we had her take the ACT when she was 12, to practice for standardized testing. Turns out that was the one and only standardized test she took (until she took the GRE at 15) and it was enough to gain entry to what would prove to be the perfect school for her. One of the things she loved about A&M was that when she sat in on a senior level neuroscience class, she barely knew anything. She was thrilled by the challenge of it all. Ironically, when she actually took that class the next year, she earned a "C." Apparently, it was indeed challenging!

Noel had been on the sprawling and beautiful Texas A&M campus several times before she was a student. We also walked around together over the summer and she attended pre-class functions during "Howdy Week." On day one, I dropped her off near her first class, with a backpack and the A&M app map on her phone. She called me in tears later in the day telling me that she had gone to the wrong building and was lost and would be late for her oceanography lab. I asked why she didn't use her app. She said she didn't want to have to need it. What can you say to that? She figured it out and made it there for the last 5 minutes of class—but at least she got the syllabus. So even experience, an app, and some supposed common sense did not help her that first day of school. But she recovered from her mistake and powered through her tears to make it all work out. That level of maturity is something you only know you have when it is tested. I wasn't worried per se, but I was glad to know she managed just fine. And yes, missing the first day of a lab is okay.

Other than the getting lost part, she had a wonderful first day, which included an email from the Honors College department stating there was a professor looking to interview/meet with honors students for a fascinating research opportunity the next evening at 6 p.m. So, on day two, we go to the west campus to attempt to find the correct building and room for this meeting. I now appreciate how easy it is to get lost on a large campus with people all around and exacting timetables! We no doubt looked befuddled as we walked around this more obscure area of campus when a kindly looking young man asked us if we need help. A Southern Gentleman, how chivalrous! When we told him the building name she needs, he told us it was around the side of the building and offered to walk her to it. And off they went. The plan was for me to just hang around the area as it was a lovely evening and how long could this meeting take anyways? It was at 6 p.m., people would want to have dinner, so who would have thought this meeting would go on for long? [cue foreboding music]

In the meantime, I sit and enjoy the fresh air and a cell phone chat with a friend. After about an hour, I wonder why she hasn't returned or texted. I get a little frustrated and anxious when I realize she has left her cell phone in the car, seemingly for the sole reason of giving me a heart attack as she usually carries her cell phone everywhere (what teenager doesn't?!). I then look for the building and find the room where the meeting was to take place. I tiptoe past, not wanting to embarrass her: it is empty. I assume she is now lost and trying to find her way back to me. I start running around the outside of this large building complex looking for her. After a few laps, I still haven't seen her and I go into full panic mode, extrapolating that the friendly-looking student who helped her must be a serial killer and has no doubt already murdered her and hidden her body somewhere nearby. I'm not saying I'm high strung, but at this point, I am literally praying that she didn't suffer as she died. I call the campus police. A nice officer arrives right away. I explain the situation. I am not at all hysterical, but not exactly in a particularly Zen place, either. He assumes I am a bit crazy because how could my daughter be 14 and be a college student? I show him her ID. He calls his sergeant. The sergeant arrives and I repeat myself. He calls for backup. It has now been 2 ½ hours and there are four cops and three patrol cars. They start calling the emergency contact for the building, who would have the professor's contact information. I show them pictures of Noel and describe the clothes she was wearing. I'm now bracing myself for the worst.

Now, let's start over from Noel's perspective, a.k.a rational world where normal things are happening...

I'm navigating an old, empty building with this random student. We find the room relatively quickly and he departs with only my "thanks!" as reward. The meeting begins, and as professors sometimes do, this guy talks for a very, very long time about his work. Pretty quickly after the start of the meeting, he decides that he has lost interest in explaining it to us and wants to actually show us, so we are escorted to his lab. In the lab, he keeps talking. That thing happens where we all know we're supposed to leave and that it's been too long, but the conversation keeps starting back up again. We're trying to wrap up and he's still going. We're putting our emails down on a list so he can contact us and he's still talking. We're literally halfway out the door and he keeps pulling us back in verbally. At some point, I give up. I've told him multiple times that I, and the rest of us, have to leave but he keeps forgetting. "I'm leaving right now, whether you're done talking or not," I announce. Everyone's faces drop, except the professor's: he *loves* it. He laughs, apologizes for rambling, and finally lets us leave without having to walk out on him mid-sentence.

I felt bad about being out so late, knowing my mom was probably a little worried, very hungry, and bored. I and a few others who had all left at the same time now attempt to navigate the empty building. We find a set of glass doors to the outside and see my mother (which is humiliating) and a few police officers (which is confusing and faintly terrifying) on the other side. We try the door and it's locked. They immediately begin screaming "PRESS THE BUTTON." We see a big red button to the side of the door: no label, no sign, just a button on the wall. A kid goes to press it but hesitates, because pressing a giant red button is a bit intimidating, despite the encouraging screams from the police: "PRESS THE BUTTON!" We do, the door unlocks, we get outside, and the other students start thanking the cops, without articulating what they're actually thanking them for, because no one knows why the cops are here, or who this lady is and why she's here. Except me. As soon as I saw them, I knew. But the other students went on their way and were none-the-wiser.

I had left my phone as I didn't want to be distracted at this meeting. Such a simple misunderstanding and yet it turned into a Hollywood thriller by the end of it.

The good news was that Mom got a workout from running around the buildings multiple times, the police knew what I looked like and believed us that I was a college student (handy in case of an actual emergency), and we have some initial plans sketched out for my untimely funeral (also handy in case of a very serious actual emergency). We decided that from now on, we would *both* have our phones on us at all times. I quickly forgave Mom for calling the cops and she forgave me for not telling her that I was leaving my phone behind: mostly, no harm, mostly no foul.

Despite the dramatic beginning, I ended up joining that research team and it was an incredible opportunity that, among other benefits, prepared me for leading my own research team at A&M a year later. If nothing else, I learned an important lesson: when in doubt, the professor will talk too long.

Looking Back with Myiesha: Beginning Early College

This story begins with Haley as an eighth-grader. She is doing well, adjusting to life as a teen in the various ways teens adjust. Transitioning from childhood to adulthood is not easy. I am reading a few books I highly recommend that (I believe) are helping me be a better person and parent: *The Conscious Parent* by Tsabary, and *A Parent's Guide to Gifted Children* by Webb Gore et al.

Raising adults requires you to be open, honest, and willing to make adjustments and learn about yourself. It also requires that the parent sees the child as the child actually is—as a full, complete, personality. These two books are helping me keep my eye on that beacon.

At this time, I had recently had Haley IQ tested, and the psychologist had these recommendations:

- Haley should continue with her extracurricular activities.

- ❍ Techniques such as curriculum-based assessment should be utilized so that Haley can progress through the curriculum as she masters it.
- ❍ Acceleration, as well as enrichment activities, should be considered.
- ❍ Early college admission should be considered. The Texas Academy of Mathematics and Science might be an option.
- ❍ Haley should be considered for placement with the Davidson Institute, as her IQ falls within the "Profoundly Gifted" range.

I felt a little behind the curve: what took me so long to go ahead and have her tested? I spent quite a bit time communicating with other parents about all things "homeschooling" in the various groups of which I am a part. One person, in particular, was super helpful, and based on what I shared about Haley, recommended I have her tested: "She sounds like a PG kid." She gave me the contact information for a local examiner. When the results came back, my hubby and I had to rethink our entire plan for her education and enrichment. The psychologist recommended keeping Haley as active as possible to stimulate her brain. She endorsed early college for Haley for the academic rigor and sense of progression and accomplishment. She warned that if we failed to keep her progressing forward, she may suffer from adverse emotional and psychological issues. She recommended the Davidson Institute and its program for profoundly gifted children—Davidson Young Scholars. So, like any good mom, I joined even *more* groups. We joined Davidson.

The Davidson Young Scholars program is a great resource because they promote understanding of gifted education and allowed me to realize just how much "damage" schools are doing to the brightest children—wasting their potential.

It reinforced our decision to homeschool and helped me articulate (better) why individualized education is so important—especially for children who are non-uniform.

One issue I've learned about is "asynchronous development" and I realize that I have misunderstood Haley in this regard. Having learned about this concept, I am beginning to really see its effects and make modifications. Overall, I am proud of her and feel that we are on target.

The journey to early college began [cue the flutes]…"oh...so very long ago" with a mother who had a "bossy" little girl with no real friends from school and a mind that moved much faster than she could handle. She was talkative and snarky. She did "good enough" academically but wasn't excelling in a way that her mother knew she could and should.

I spent time with Haley going over relatively complex concepts in 5th grade (as a supplement to her intermediate school science). She gobbled up concepts such as the cardiac cycle, embryology, and action potentials in the nervous system with an almost full understanding after a single explanation.

That could mean one of two things: Either I was an awesome teacher, or she was a brilliant student. It was likely a combination of both.

As she began acquiescing to the expectations of the institution, I could see the light dimming in her eyes and I knew I had to do something. I started by trying to argue *within* the system: teacher changes, challenges to school leadership, Gifted and Talented coordinators, and working with other parents. Ultimately, I realized that the system *itself* was the problem. I decided to refocus my time and efforts away from trying to change an unwieldy institutional system to fit my child. When I directed the same time, energy, stress, and effort directly in doing my best for my child (rather than undoing a system), I realized it was better spent.

In retrospect, I realize that what we did was essentially to pull Haley out of intermediate school, had her skip middle school, and begin high-school at age 10. Haley would have been starting 6th grade, had we not pulled her out. My rationale for doing so at that juncture was that if it didn't work out, I could just put her back into public school seamlessly as a "repeat 6th grader" (who would then be age 11 starting 6th grade for the 2nd time, by which time all of her friends at school would have moved on to middle school and off-campus). I convinced myself that pulling her out was a win-win situation and easily fixed if necessary down the road.

However, once Haley was out of traditional school, she was able to move at her own rate, which turned out to be extremely fast.

For us, this path was convoluted because I had to adjust, and readjust my thoughts, plans, and ideas constantly. And along the way, many great oracles taught me how to read the "tea-leaves" of giftedness. Everything seemed to happen by happenstance. The only constant that I was sure of was that my girl was doing well and that we were therefore on the right path. Even if the curves in that path were unpredictable.

For instance, she was motivated to take the ACT. I was against it. Why take it? For what purpose? But she insisted. A homeschool buddy in Hybrid School was taking it, and she wanted to have that experience as well. She took a practice ACT and did very well. Much to my surprise. Her ultimate score gained her entry into the Talent Searches and their programs.

Likewise, she was motivated to take geometry on her own during the summer. She took an entire year of geometry (that's 107 lessons) in twelve weeks! With the help of a tutor, she did it. Who was I to hold her back?

Around this time, I met Nancy in my new Davidson Young Scholar circle. She had recently shared that Noel was a recent graduate of Texas A&M and was a Ph.D. student at UNT. She offered to meet with me and Haley to talk over ice-cream. After meeting Noel, marveling over her ability to express herself, her passion, and seeing how awesome a 16-year-old can be, I was motivated to learn more about early college. This meeting, combined with the recommendation from our psychologist, prompted me to take a visit to our local community college—just to gather some information.

After meeting with an excellent advisor there, I brought Haley and Dad back so we could discuss a plan and maybe take one class. I was thinking either an art class (something fun) or a math class, because after a couple of years of homeschooling Haley was now a math whiz and wanted to major in math in college! She participated in the Awesome Math Program in Plano, Texas, and found the math a fascinating and fun challenge. There were no arbitrary rules about how you could, or couldn't, solve the problems based on a state exam. And she took the AMC 10 (American Mathematics Competition) and scored in the top 25% of young test-takers worldwide. She needed higher math, and the hybrid school could not provide it. So I wanted to investigate the community college option for upper-division math.

I fretted over my decision to have her start college at age 13 and meditated on the idea. I even consulted this helpful publication: *Considering the Options: A Guidebook for Investigating Early College Entrance.* (Written by Nancy M. Robinson and The Davidson Institute, in case you want to check it out yourself.)

After consulting with my husband, talking to Haley, reading the book, meeting with other parents, speaking to Nancy and Noel, and understanding the asynchrony in her development as evidenced by some of her behaviors, interests, and grades (study habits, follow-through, diligence, etc.) I felt like Haley needed more time. She could *do* the work, academically. But she'd require support. There's no way she'll be ready to "do it on her own" in time for college away from home next year (or the year following). She needed time "figure things out" with regards to her study habits, decision making, prioritization, etc. She still required too much oversight and executive management to be successful.

Going away to college was not an option, but I didn't want to take anything off the table. If she started college early, she would not be able to go to an Ivy, or an HBCU (Historically Black College or University) as I did. She would not earn a fencing scholarship and she would be relegated to local colleges and universities. That is a huge consideration.

Now we had a new dilemma on our hands: do we preserve college options by holding her back in high school or do we allow her to start college early, forego those other great options, but allow her to progress at her own pace and complete her academic training on her own timeline? If we don't allow her to start college early, what will we do about her school and education? How will she enjoy the challenges and progression that she thrives on if we keep her in the "high-school box" because of her age?

We did not want to limit her or clip her proverbial wings... but was she ready for college at 13?

As a homeschool mom with a science degree, I decided to go ahead and give credentials to some of her knowledge. We signed her up for a College Algebra CLEP (which she passed first time with zero preparation). I went up to the Community College to investigate having her take math and science up there (which would be cheaper than the private tutors and would provide course credentials). I ruminated on the idea of dual credits vs early college admission, using the classic pros-and-cons list method.

The pros of early college? The student is challenged academically. The student is able to get started on a college degree sooner and therefore more likely to complete the degree in a timely fashion. The student has the opportunity to take more than 6-8 credit hours. The student can take remediation courses if necessary. The student is done with high school. The student is eligible for *college* programs and scholarships, etc. Credits obtained count towards a Bachelor's degree. And, finally, her classmates will be more interested and motivated in their coursework.

The cons? She would need to pass the Texas Success Initiative (TSI), which is another hoop (she ended up doing this with no problem). She may forego participation in high school opportunities like math competitions, Olympiads, and social clubs like Jack and Jill of America, Rhoers, and Mocha Moms. The grades obtained will count and go onto a college transcript and they will sit there for the rest of the child's life: that's stressful! She cannot live away from home, so her options are limited to community college (initially) and then (since she'll only be 15) to colleges/universities in the DFW metroplex. Freshman scholarships are potentially forfeited, but with the locally available options charging around $1000/month, this isn't a huge con, and there are many transfer scholarships available. Plus, there's no charge for her room and board, so those dorm and meal plan costs were minimized.

We determined that the pros outweighed the cons for us. With that major decision behind us, we had a lot of work ahead. Getting into college is big business. From independent educational strategists and college counselors to sensational news stories and high-profile lawsuits, it is clear that people are looking for a clear pathway for their children into our colleges and universities. As a homeschooler, that path offers an immediate distinction because homeschooling is very "interesting" to admissions officials. A homeschool student is already a stand-out.

From my journey, what I've learned about college admission is that the story behind the accolades matter. Creating a consistent narrative is an effective way to focus attention on your student's best attributes. As a homeschool student, I would recommend looking at the student's "most likely" school requirements for homeschool students early on—as early as middle school. It's useful to plot and plan an academic path that meets entry criteria. How many AP exams are recommended? How many SAT subject exams are required? Which classes are prerequisites (and must therefore be documented on your transcript)? Plan it out. This needs to start (even if the child is graduating at 18) by 8th grade to be competitive. The "easiest" AP test is Human Geography. Many children can self-study and then sit for this exam and pass, which can help the student obtain AP Scholar status (which requires three successful AP exams on the books with a score of 3+).

There's room to stand out in the extracurricular world as well. I had Haley play the harp which fascinated college admissions officials. I had Haley learn fencing which opened doors to elite college consideration, as recruiters were very interested in her performance. I had Haley doing speech, debate, and mock trial. I would venture a guess that these activities (harp, fencing, debate) were more eye-catching than some of their more traditional counterparts (piano, soccer, chess). While these activities played to her strengths, they were uncommon enough to be conversation pieces and interesting to people looking for stand-out students. Oftentimes, my children may not have been enthusiastic about an activity I selected for them. I explained to them that enthusiasm comes with increasing skill and dominance in an area. Winning is fun; being good at something is fun. Therefore, I was not interested in their lack of enthusiasm for an activity simply because they just felt "bad" at it. Get some practice, learn the basics, then let's talk. It's much easier to enjoy doing things you excel at. I've found that making kids put significant effort into something before deciding if they will continue teaches them resilience and patience. There's no need to force them to continue an activity they have consistently disliked or not improved at for a long period, but it's good to remind them that being bad at something is a necessary step to being good at it.

Further, consider exploring atypical routes to college. With the cost of higher education soaring and crippling student debt, it has become imperative to be strategic. Considering community college, and local state schools for non-terminal degrees may make the most logical sense. While having a college degree isn't required of all students, it doesn't hurt to have one, nor does it detract from natural gifts and trade occupational pursuits as long as the cost isn't staggering. Further, if they can complete college by age 18, they can then entertain a myriad of options ranging from vocational trade schools to graduate programs. Completing college doesn't have to be a zero-sum game or a mutually exclusive endeavor competing with trades.

Finally, the idea of a gap year is noble; however, a student that is unsure of their next steps could be better served by progressing forward. All degrees require a set of core classes. Why take a "gap year" when a student could be working on these ubiquitous core requirements at the local community college? Oftentimes in life, our paths become clearer as we maintain forward momentum. Consider a car's headlights: we don't always have to be familiar with the entire road to our destination because the headlights will light the way a few feet at a time. Our continued motion allows the headlights of our car to light up more of the path. Pulling off the road and taking a break doesn't necessarily offer any new revelations about our journey.

Chapter 10
Life in Early College

Misconceptions and Reality of College

When a young student goes to college, people sometimes assume that also entails the entire young adult experience that our society has made of college: Parties, alcohol, experimentation, and all those other quasi-adult activities. However, in the case of a young college student, college is simply a description of the level of academic work undertaken.

A young student starting early college is not necessarily going to move into a dorm or off-campus apartment and be left to fend for themselves. A young student who is ready for college-level academic challenges will likely be there to simply take the classes that challenge them and allow for advanced thinking beyond what high-school can provide. It is a relationship with professors well-versed in their fields of study, who offer advanced level course-work that can engage an enthusiastic, young mind.

Gifted children are often asynchronous in their development. A child that is able to study and understand advanced concepts in Physics may not be able to organize themselves properly to coordinate a social life or manage their own time. As a parent of an early college student, you are allowing for your child to continue learning at an advanced level in an area of interest or giftedness, while supporting them in areas of relative weakness—such as executive functioning or administrative support. As in sports, a gifted, young gymnast may not be ready for the attention, may not be able to market themselves, to coordinate their own schedule or to handle their own business. However, there is no expectation of that elite athlete to manage their entire life, but rather to focus and perfect their own performance. Likewise, the gifted and precocious early college student is not expected to have the ability to manage their entire lives as a prerequisite to advanced learning.

Using an Advisor

College advisors are excellent resources for any college student; however, selecting an appropriate advisor to support a young college student is key. It is important to interact with the college advisor via email and in-person to ascertain their responsiveness and ability to help your student navigate the chosen degree plan. College advisors are often young adults who've recently graduated from college themselves. Many are working on advanced degrees and are paid surprisingly low wages given the significance of their work. As such, it is essential that as a parent with a young student, decisions are not deferred to the advisor. The advisor's suggestions should be taken into consideration, double-checked against printed materials, such as the university catalog, and a plan of action taken based on all available data. Email correspondence is essential to both verify and document conversations between your student and their advisor. Advisors will change, and relying on verbal exchanges is always risky. Also consider that advisors may not have any knowledge in the area of study that your student is pursuing—such as post-college career options, or information on how to leverage their degree and the education received into emerging fields and markets.

The real value of a college advisor is in helping formulate a degree plan, as well as securing acceptable alternatives where needed. A discussion and subsequent email to an advisor about a course substitution or sequence of classes can be the documentation you need to ensure a timely graduation. There are occasions when degree requirements change, and unless you have written documentation and can be "grandfathered" in, you might have to take additional classes, which can result in extra expense and time

It is important to select an advisor who supports your student's goals and is willing to advocate for him or her if needed. Oftentimes, people struggle to think beyond the one way they know how to do something, and a non-traditional student can require a different approach. An advisor who is dismissive, aloof, or outright discouraging to non-traditional students should be avoided. Additionally, as a parent, it is important to have a good rapport with your child's advisor which will mean having FERPA (Family Educational Rights and Privacy Act) paperwork on file so that academic details can be openly discussed.

Selecting a Major

Selecting a major can be a source of great anxiety for many students and parents. Less than a third of college graduates have a job related to their major, and nearly a third change their majors prior to graduating (ACT, 2008; Washington Post, 2013; Lederman, 2013). So really how important is it to select the perfect college major?

For a young student, the college major is not nearly as important because the chances are high that the student is not yet aware of all of their options, nor have they developed their world-view sufficiently to fully engage in life-work choices as teenagers. With the information you have at the time, select a degree plan that seems both interesting and plays to the strengths of the student. As a young student, there is time to get advanced training in areas of true interest by way of certificates, second bachelor degrees, master's degrees, doctorates, and/or professional degrees. Starting college early, and selecting an "interest" major detracts nothing from the young early college student. At age 18, when most students are receiving a high-school diploma, your student may receive a bachelor's in arts or science. This is a huge accomplishment, no matter the major.

Some professional schools, such as medical school, require a specific set of classes that must be taken in a specific sequence. For a young student, caution must be taken that a college transcript isn't tarnished by a low grade in an introductory science class that will live on in their GPA in perpetuity. This may affect early graduation from college because those specific science courses may need to be taken over a longer period of time. However, early entry into college does not have to be delayed. Entrance into college can mean completing the core classes, and later semesters can be dedicated to graduate school preparation. Post-graduate work is also a great way to gain maturity, ascertain if a career path is desirable or not, and practice your performance in that field of interest. Post-graduate work is preferable to changing majors, or otherwise stagnating and waiting for the "perfect" path or outcome.

When the student is at community college, it's important to investigate likely schools he or she hopes to attend next (either as a transfer, or as a freshman with dual-enrollment credits), as well as the desired degree plan. This will help you avoid wasting time and unnecessary coursework. While general exploration of courses may be helpful, depending on state laws, taking too many courses that do not meet degree requirements could prove detrimental and even incur penalties such as increased tuition and forfeiture of other financial aid and scholarships.

Dual-Enrollment

Dual-enrollment (DE) is where a student is simultaneously enrolled in high school and college. It is an often underutilized, underappreciated money saver and can offer a competitive advantage to students looking to attend an elite school. But equally important, DE can serve as a valuable tool for students looking to complete college early. DE can take many forms, including college-level classes taught on high-school campuses or in homeschool-hybrid schools. And certainly, it can also include high-school students taking a college class on a college or university campus.

A student can take a plethora of DE courses under the umbrella of "high-school" education and not be penalized in their college applications or admissions (as in, they get to stay a true Freshman and qualify for Freshman scholarships). However, it only takes one college course taken as a non-DE student, and all of those previous DE courses come out from under the DE umbrella and become "college coursework."

What does this mean in practice? This means that a student who takes 60 units of college courses as DE can still be considered a freshman and enjoy the many advantages therein. After one semester at a university (when those DE credits come out from under the DE umbrella), they could have 75+ college credits and go from Freshman status to Junior status after one college semester. If the vast majority of those credits meet degree plan criteria, suddenly college can be a 2-3 year experience instead of lasting 4-5 years.

Finally, another advantage to DE or community college coursework after homeschooling is that many colleges have programs that support an automatic acceptance of a student on completion of a certain number of college credits. Transfer scholarships are abundant, and Phi Theta Kappa (the international community college honor society) has very real and significant scholarship opportunities available to students who opt to graduate from high-school early and transfer to a university from a community college.

The Value of a College Degree

With the rising cost of college tuition, expanding debt burdens, and ambiguous job prospects, many may question the value of a college degree. However, it is widely acknowledged that a college degree, and the knowledge acquired at the university level, is essential for most professional jobs and careers. Therefore, reflection on college and its value should rather center on the cost of attendance, selection of a major, ultimate career goals, and a consideration of early college.

The cost of college attendance has skyrocketed and increased at a rate that outpaces inflation. This fact is frequently voiced as a reason to forego college. However, it is important to acknowledge that there are many affordable public colleges and strategies to reduce costs—such as community college, exam by credit (such as CLEP), and institutions that award merit and need-based financial aid once they see the value of your student. It is easy for parents and students to become enamored of fancy expensive colleges and universities for superficial reasons. Staying focused on what's important—advanced learning and getting a degree—allows you to select institutions that are within your budget and are more likely to result in timely graduation. No doubt, an elite university may well be worth what you pay for it, but those schools also turn away many extraordinary and exceptional applicants every year. Pinning your hopes on a fancy school with a plethora of scholarship money has left many a student heartbroken.

Understanding the purpose of college helps parents and students stay focused on their goal. Oftentimes, the entry point into professional careers is via a college degree. If a student is unsure of their ultimate career goals, a college degree allows them to keep their options open and push them into an environment where they can explore those options. As such, "not knowing what you want to do" is a great reason to consider college. A college degree is something that is great to have, even if you don't need it immediately. Realizing a college degree is necessary later in life can be a major obstacle—especially for young women as they try to balance the many aspects of having a family and/or a career.

Selecting an institution/program that doesn't create significant debt or drain family resources is ideal. Generally, a student with aspirations to obtain a graduate or professional degree should avoid excessive debt on their undergraduate, non-terminal degree. In so doing, the value of the college education increases exponentially. It is always a financial risk to go into a graduate program with undergraduate debt, especially for a younger student.

Compulsory education laws keep most students in school until at least the age of 16. At the end of the standard K-12 curriculum, students are awarded a high-school diploma. While students with that diploma fare better than their counterparts who did not graduate high-school, the value of a Bachelor's degree surely trumps a high-school diploma. If a student can achieve their Bachelor's degree by age 18, they are maximizing the use of their time in compulsory education.

In short, the student is going to school anyway: they may as well get the college degree.

Further, a young woman getting a college degree early has other added benefits. Women still carry the majority of the responsibility for child-care, elder-care, and home management. Women make less money than their male counterparts, in part, because of the "motherhood penalty" (Bright Futures, 2018). Women have added stressors, and extra considerations regarding family planning and work-life balance. Obtaining a college degree at a younger age can relieve some of this pressure.

Young and in College

When most people think of early college, visions of drunken parties and rampant drug use come to mind. The entire social, adult experimentation scene predominates our ideas about what it means to be a college student. With a young student, however, the motivation for college attendance is simplified. An academically and/or intellectually gifted child may quite literally run out of classes to take in an academic discipline if they are not at a college or university. The structure, expertise, and organization of a college course under the instruction of a professor with expertise in a chosen field is not easily imitated or recreated outside of higher education. The mindset that accompanies an early college entrant is one based more on educational considerations than the "college experience."

Often there is concern about a young student interacting with older students. Study sessions at a library are easy enough to envision; frat parties, not so much. Like all parenting, communication is key, and safety is paramount. Good things and bad things happen every day (and night) on every high school and college campus. Whereas, one student-parent combination may feel more comfortable with a parent on campus, another may be okay with just regular text updates and yet another will be more hands off. Again, YMMV. The takeaway is to have clear communication about the why and how of early college, and quite frankly, college in general.

Other early college concerns center around "maturity" and the child's ability to have the life-skills needed to succeed. However, it is not necessary for anyone—especially a young student—to have the capacity to manage all of their life affairs in order to take advantage of an early college option. It is not unusual for parents and coaches of elite and advanced youngsters in a variety of areas to have executive support, continued guidance, help with time management, administrative assistance, and overall facilitation of other daily life functions while focusing on their area of advancement—be that gymnastics or mathematics. There is no justification for halting the academic growth and development of a student because there are deficits in other areas of self-expression. We don't prevent elite actors or athletes from engaging in their art or sport because they don't know how to plan their own rehearsal schedule. Likewise, it is disingenuous to hold academically gifted scholars to a standard of overall maturity that is not on par for their age; they should instead be allowed to develop and grow in their unique areas of giftedness.

Another consideration when thinking about college is to look at the Common College App or the application for a University your child could attend. Think about what questions they are asking. Just as you prepare for a job interview, you should consider common questions such as, "Talk about a time you had to work as a team" or "Talk about a time you had to handle conflict at the office." You can look at those college applications and think about what the college is asking of your student. This might help you think about college from a different point of view and help make your decisions a bit easier. Conversely, you may find you dislike that mindset, and want to do what feels more organic. That is absolutely awesome as well. Remember, there are almost 5000 colleges in the United States, and over 22,000, worldwide. There are options out there!

When going outside the norm for an education, you may interact with people who have never thought outside the box and their default answer is "No." Comments such as "We've never done that before" or "But, he/she is so young" should be opportunities to respond with "Awesome! A chance to do something different" and "Isn't it fantastic?" Tact, diplomacy, and a smile can often go a long way in such situations. So can knowing your rights. There are laws on the books to prohibit age discrimination. If you encounter unhelpful people, a good response is, "Where is that written down?" or "Where is the statute/law that prohibits this?" Kill them with kindness, but also remember to exhaust every avenue to do what is best for your child. The first unhelpful individual you encounter is only that, the first. There is usually more than one person with the authority or ability to help you. There are already protocols in place for taking the SAT and ACT earlier than the norm. So, if you run into an organization, whether private or public, that has no such protocols, you can help make that happen for your kid, and the kids that come after you. Or at least give it your best shot.

You may be hit with "What if it isn't a good fit?" The reply to this comment is, "What do you do when it isn't a good fit for other students?" You, as the parent, are generally in the best place to know what is best for your child. If not, we would live in some Dystopian world where the government raised our children for us from birth. Of course, there are some reasons a young child should *not* be in a classroom with older students. The course material may be inappropriate for their age—a subjective decision that only a parent can make. The other students may be unkind—any worse than middle school bullies? Your child may not be mature enough—this, however, is a very real issue. Can your child stay focused, take notes, and manage themselves comparable to everyone else? Can they ask questions respectfully and be respectful to other students? These are legitimate concerns. If you believe your child can do those things and wants those things, why not try them out?

Another challenge you may face by bucking the status quo is people pushing back on your child missing out on what are considered key cultural events of certain phases of our lives in America: Prom, homecoming, frat parties, etc. If you were the valedictorian, homecoming queen, the varsity cheerleader with a myriad of friends and amazing experiences in high school—fantastic! We can well imagine why you would want that for your kid, assuming they are a carbon copy of you and want those same things. If so, go for it! But perhaps you should weigh the value of being academically challenged and fulfilled vs. potentially being on the Homecoming Court. Again, if you can make that work with a traditional public education, count yourself lucky and enjoy the ride. If not, you have to make some hard choices.

Other parental concerns

Any time we send our children out into the world, there is worry and concern. Even kindergarteners are subjected to "active shooter drills" in public and private schools which serve as a stark reminder of the vulnerability we all feel. There is no way of getting around worrying about your kid.

When they leave for college it causes a great deal of anxiety. As parents, we are aware of the myriad of dangers that seem to lurk around every corner. We are aware of the potentially life-altering decisions that are frequently made by young people that will either further their assent to happiness and success or jeopardize all their hopes and dreams for their future.

The number one cause of death in young people ages 15 - 24 is unintentional injury (which are various types of accidents and trauma). Numbers two and three are suicide and homicide, respectively. In fact, the number one cause of death is unintentional injury all the way up to age 44 (CDC, 2015; Curtin, 2018). Therefore, your concern as a parent for their safety and well-being at the most basic level is very much warranted.

However, there are two questions that should be asked when considering the safety and well-being of an early college student:

1. Is the child more at risk than a slightly older person of adverse situations on a college campus, and if so how?

2. How can risks to all students be mitigated, and what are the particular extra precautions that should be taken if the student is under the age of 18?

There is a concern that a young child will be exposed to "adult experiences," such as sex and drugs. However, the average age of first marijuana use is age 14 (AACAP, 2018). By their senior year "almost 70 percent of high school students will have tried alcohol, half will have taken an illegal drug, nearly 40 percent will have smoked a cigarette, and more than 20 percent will have used a prescription drug for a nonmedical purpose" (NIDA, 2014).

Vaping is wreaking havoc on the lungs of our children with a spike in adverse outcomes and deaths. "Among 8th-grade students, nicotine vaping in the past 30 days increased 2.6 percentage points from 3.5% to 6.1%. This is the second-largest increase ever recorded for this grade." (University of Michigan, 2018)

The average age of first sexual experience in America is seventeen for both boys and girls (CDC, 2017a). Further, over 60% of young women and men have had sex by age 19 (CDC, 2017b). Digital porn and exposure to the risks of sexual manipulation is heightened for children and is a major problem.

There are a multitude of issues that should concern any parent.

However, our children's exposure to these "adult situations" happens way before they turn 18. This is important to note for a couple of reasons. First, even if the child is at home with you, they are more likely than not to engage in (or have exposure to) many of these "adult situations." Second, going to college at 18 offers no special protection. Actually, with the expectation of more independence and freedom bestowed upon a student at age 18, parental influence is markedly diminished. Therefore, helping your child navigate these inevitable "adult situations" is also diminished. Further, holding off college for a student that is academically ready does not serve to avoid these situations but rather just delays their academic development.

Adolescence is a time of rapid brain rewiring. (Arain, Haque, et al., 2013) It is "a period of vulnerability for mental illness, when environmental factors interact with genetic and neurodevelopmental factors to lead to health or illness in adulthood." (Psychology Today,

2018) This is true to the extent that that "50% of all lifetime mental illnesses develop by age 14 and 75% develop by age 24." (NAMI, 2019) At the very time in their lives when young people are at their most vulnerable, we send them away from us to "fly alone" in stressful academic environments while trying to learn to navigate society as an adult. For many gifted students who are both motivated and intense, this can be a recipe for disaster. To mitigate this, allowing them to progress academically while under the watchful eye and support of a nurturing family structure can help create an environment that supports mental and emotional health.

To answer our first question "Is your child more at risk than an average 18-year-old college student?" The answer is no. All children have significant areas of concern, many that are actually unique to older adolescents.

However, there are some unique challenges a young college student will face. This is where we address question number two: "How can risks to all students be mitigated, and what are the particular extra precautions that should be taken if the student is under the age of 18?"

Staying Safe(r)

Obviously there are some young students who are not emotionally, socially, or developmentally equipped to sit in a college-level class and cooperate or participate in a meaningful way. To be successful, a student needs to be able to follow directions, take notes, and be able to ask and answer questions posed to and by the professor. The child needs to be trustworthy, and openly communicative with their parents. Finally, the child needs to have the ability to control their impulses. If a student does not possess these attributes, they will struggle regardless of their age.

Once it has been determined that the child is capable of being in a classroom setting as an engaged participant, and can be trusted to do what's expected of them, their safety on campus is similar to any other student. The difference between a 14-year old girl's safety on campus and an 18-year-old girl's safety on campus is her decision-making capacity and ability to learn to avoid dangerous situations. There is no "magical protection" afforded to an 18- or 22-year old body. As such, good decision-making should be supported by involved and vigilant parents to enhance campus safety of young students.

An important point to emphasize in the early college discussion and college campus safety is the distinction between simply taking college classes vs total immersion in college life. A young student can attend classes, engage in school activities, join clubs, run for leadership office, all while staying at home and commuting to and from school. This allows full participation in very controlled settings (classrooms, study groups, club meetings) while limiting the unsupervised social experiences that tend to lead to trouble (parties, loitering, and "hanging out"). In this way, the young student reaps the benefits of being a college student, but the dangers are mitigated. The dangers of traditional high school, in this regard, are not dissimilar from these same issues at college-level.

Though it comes with its own challenges, life in early college can be an improvement on traditional college life in many ways. The values and priorities of families and students certainly vary from home to dorm to frat house. Generally, conversations and expectations are more easily had with minors than with an adult student. You have to make the decision that's right for you (hint: this is sort of the thesis of the entire book...so I hope you noticed this idea before now), but do your best to reach that decision starting from a place of open-mindedness and empiricism rather than fearful dramatization. Everything sounds terrifying if you imagine the worst-case scenario: most of the things people are scared of happening in an early college atmosphere are just as likely, if not significantly more likely, to happen in high school. For some families, including ours, the benefits outweighed the risks so enormously that it was not even *that* difficult of a decision, even if it was at times a scary or strange one. However, we did come from our own cultural backgrounds which, despite their differences, encouraged academic success more than others' might. All that matters in the end is that you consider early college by comparing your situation to the *reality* of early college, rather than the fear-fueled nightmare version that is sometimes spread among naysayers.

References

ACT (2018). *National CCCR.* Retrieved from: https://www.act.org/content/dam/act/unsecured/documents/cccr2018/National-CCCR-2018.pdf

American Academy of Child & Adolescent Psychiatry (2018). *Teens: Alcohol and Other Drugs No. 3.* Retrieved from: https://www.aacap.org/AACAP/Families and Youth/Facts for Families/FFF-Guide/Teens-Alcohol-And-Other-Drugs-003.aspx

Arain, M., Haque, M. et al. (2013) Maturation of the adolescent brain. *Neuropsychiatric Disease and Treatment. 9*: 449–461

Bright Horizons (2018). *Modern Family Index: Motherhood Penalty.* Retrieved from: https://www.brighthorizons.com/-/media/bh-new/newsroom/media-kit/mfi 2018 report final.ashx

Centers for Disease Control and Prevention (2015) *10 Leading Causes of Death by Age Group, United States.* Retrieved from: https://www.cdc.gov/injury/wisqars/pdf/leading causes of death by age group 2015-a.pdf

Centers for Disease Control and Prevention (2017a). *Key Statistics from the National Survey of Family Growth - S Listing.* Retrieved from: https://www.cdc.gov/nchs/nsfg/key statistics/s.htm

Centers for Disease Control and Prevention (2017b). *Key Statistics from the National Survey of Family Growth - T Listing.* Retrieved from: https://www.cdc.gov/nchs/nsfg/key statistics/t.htm

Curtin, S. Heron, M. et al. (2018) *Recent Increases in Injury Mortality Among Children and Adolescents Aged 10 - 19 Years in the United States: 1999-2016.* National Vital Statistics Report. June 1, 2018. Retrieved from: https://www.cdc.gov/nchs/data/nvsr/nvsr67/nvsr67 04.pdf

Inside Higher Ed (2017). *Nearly a third of students change major within three years.* Retrieved from: https://www.insidehighered.com/news/2017/12/08/nearly-third-students-change-major-within-three-years-math-majors-most

National Institute on Drug Abuse (2014). *Principles of Adolescent Substance Use Disorder Treatment: A Research-Based Guide.* Retrieved from: https://www.drugabuse.gov/publications/principles-adolescent-substance-use-disorder-treatment-research-based-guide/introduction

National Alliance on Mental Illness (2019). *Teens and Young Adults.* Retrieved from: https://www.nami.org/Find-Support/Teens-and-Young-Adults

Psychology Today (2018). *What Underlying Brain Dysconnectivity Causes Mental Illness?* Retrieved from: https://www.psychologytoday.com/us/blog/psychiatry-the-people/201802/what-underlying-brain-dysconnectivity-causes-mental-illness

University of Michigan Institute for Social Research (2018). *National Adolescent Drug Trends in 2018.* Retrieved from: http://www.monitoringthefuture.org/pressreleases/18drugpr.pdf

Washington Post (2013). *Only 27 percent of grads have a job related to their major.* Retrieved from: https://www.washingtonpost.com/news/wonk/wp/2013/05/20/only-27-percent-of-college-grads-have-a-job-related-to-their-major/?noredirect=on&utm_term=.170903585783

Looking Back with Noel: Hate Comments—A Love Story

One of the more common fears among "child prodigies" (I feel so awkward labelling myself as a part of this group, though it beats what people have started calling me lately—*former* child prodigy) is press. To do interviews or not to do interviews, that is the question. I personally enjoyed doing interviews, though I was somewhat selective about who I talked to. I mainly did it because I felt like so many people didn't realize this was even possible, and I wanted to spread that knowledge—shocking, I know, considering I'm writing this book about it!

When the very first article about me posted, just after I graduated with my Bachelor's from Texas A&M in 2015, I happened to be up late to see it go live on Facebook. For a few minutes, there were just a few likes and a dozen views, and it was a very surreal moment, but then it was interrupted by the very first comment:

"She a hoe."

I'm not joking. That was the first comment on my first piece of press, word for word. I remember it vividly. I didn't know the guy who posted it, so he had no evidence I was a hoe. More to the point, I am not and never have been a ho nor a hoe, so there would be no evidence for his claim. But I loved it! It was hilarious. I got many more comments in the next few days, and the hate comments after "she a hoe" (though generally rare) were much more painful and personal, but I think starting off with such a random, baseless, absurd one helped me realize I would need to avoid taking them seriously.

Here are a few highlights from and responses to the comments on my press over the past years. Hopefully, they will offer an idea of some the main themes:

"I met her once...she still has some growing up to do."

Yes, obviously, that's a pretty typical aspect of being 16 and literally not fully grown up. Meanwhile, my former Intro to Philosophy classmate in her 20s has no growing up to do, apparently.

"But what about experiencing her adolescence?"

I experienced it, just during college.

"Psychology? What a waste of time!"

As the author of that first article about me responded, "Yeah, helping people is stupid!"

"Privileged, not gifted."

Privileged and gifted. I have had some great opportunities afforded to me that others have not. I also lived in a trailer for part of my youth and missed out on plenty of other opportunities because of a lack of funds. I was also bullied, excluded, and belittled in many communities, even for the gifted, because I was the only girl. You win some and you lose some. Privilege isn't enough to get you into college five years ahead of schedule.

"I want her to be my sugar mama!"

See the aforementioned poverty thing, sorry I can't help you there.

"Sheldon Cooper!" or "Doogie Howser!"

I appreciate that these characters help people relate to me, but I wish I didn't have to be reduced to a stereotype in order to be understood. It doesn't help that Sheldon is generally rude and socially inept...it's really not a flattering comparison.

But of course, in the end, the best comments are the ones like these:

"This is so amazing. Go you! I'm going to show my daughter this right now!"

"My son is two years skipped in Math. So glad to see smart kids being talked about."

"#girlpower"

"We were so afraid to skip any grades or go to college early, this is comforting."

"Congrats to her!"

My confidence doesn't rely on encouragement from positive online comments, but it does remind me why I put up with the other comments. It reminds me who I am doing this for. I never pursued press, I only allowed it, and I had no intention of glorifying myself but simply raising awareness for my community. It is tiring to see those hateful comments. It is hurtful when you realize that people think you are stealing your success from someone else; they think you're cheating in a zero-sum game or something. But progress takes time, and I do believe that people are learning how to be happy for others instead of taking their accomplishments as a personal affront. That said, I wouldn't know for sure, because I don't read the comments anymore.

Looking Back with Nancy: Acne and Academia

When Noel was a newly minted 13-year old college student, she was more worried about acne than academics. She wanted to see a dermatologist; I wanted her to work longer with an over-the-counter product, but I acquiesced and we made an appointment. At this time, she was volunteering on Monday evenings at a homeless shelter through our church high school youth group. The doctor's appointment was on a Wednesday morning. The doctor quickly wrote a prescription for acne and asked if there was anything else to discuss while we were there. Noel then mentioned that the back of her neck and head had been a little itchy. That was news to me. The doctor put on a glove, as she seemingly knew what was coming, and had Noel flip her long hair over her head. The doctor casually mentioned "lice", as one of those disgusting parasites fell onto Noel's pants. Noel let out a scream. I screamed internally. Noel started to cry, and I figured only one of us gets to cry and she beat me to it. *Where? When? Now what? When did it start itching and where were we the last few days?* Noel said she gave piggyback rides to some of the kids at the shelter, otherwise she had not been close to anyone's head or shared a comb or hat, etc. We guessed that was the source. After the doctor explained protocols and tips to stop it from spreading, I remembered she had class in a few hours. I ask when she can go to school. The doctor says she will write a note. I repeat that I don't need a note, explaining that she is a college student in a compressed semester (she started college in mid-March with two classes in an 8-week semester vs. the normal 16-week option) and missing class would be a serious hardship, since each class meets for twice the amount of time each session. The doctor looks flummoxed.

The doctor looked at the chart and says, "But, wait. She's 13."

As Noel continues sobbing and I try to hide my panic, my fear, and my own long hair, I say, "Yes, she is 13 and taking college classes."

The doctor then turned to Noel, and said passionately, soberly, "Oh, you have to cure cancer! My nephew has cancer and you have to cure it!"

I was floored; Noel was still sobbing but hesitantly promised to try. I just wanted to get out of there and start dealing with the lice. But sure, after we deal with the lice and the acne, Noel will turn tail to curing cancer.

Of course, the doctor had good intentions. But a sobbing 13-year-old with parasites crawling on her head, who has little interest in medicine per se, should certainly *not* have the weight of curing cancer on her shoulders. Thanks, Doc. That's *totally* reasonable.

This story is like many I have heard over the years. Sadly, bullies are not always other children, and every once in a blue moon an insecure, annoying, or aggressive adult will come along and put you and/or your child in an uncomfortable situation. It is such a difficult paradox that we must teach our kids to be respectful of everyone, especially adults, but also help them stand up for themselves and navigate awkward situations.

With homeschooling, for example, we learned that when an adult asked what grade she was in, they really didn't want to hear a complex answer, just basically how old she was. Was it annoying to constantly be asked what grade you're in, when you know you can't give a good answer? Yes, and that was something she simply had to accept. As their parent, you have to find that balance where you support your child without accidentally teaching them that the best response to rude comments is increased aggression. There are benefits to this approach, sure, but oftentimes we find ourselves so stunned that we don't even have time to properly react. In the end, this is probably for the best, since we want to remain calm and take the high road whenever possible.

You have to work with your kid to find the line between acceptable and unacceptable ignorance: I wish I could tell you exactly where to set that line, and what to do when it is crossed, but I can't. What I can say is that stories like these can be stressful when they occur, but they are often funny and ridiculous in retrospect. After all, here we are using this incident as a teaching moment (and hopefully some light entertainment) for you today!

Chapter 11
Career, Trades, Grad School and Beyond

Trade Schools

The cultural shift that diminished the status of trade schools and vocational training and pushed the idea that everyone should go to college is tragic. It is one of those grand ideas that has had substantial collateral damage, as grand ideas often do. Students are stressed out, and families over-extended trying to pay for expensive colleges that they can't afford in an effort to secure what they feel is a "better future" for their child. The pressure to get into the "most prestigious" college without regard for other important factors has resulted in much pain and suffering for parents and students, and notably even in criminal charges against rich celebrities.

Although it is, of course, true that college should be an option for everyone, it doesn't mean everyone will benefit from going to college or will be successful. The latest research indicates that a staggering 30% of freshmen drop out after their first year. Whether they were not academically or emotionally ready is up for debate. Regardless, that is a tremendous waste of time and energy for everyone. Not to mention the emotional and monetary strain on the student and the family.

No doubt, there is much to be gained from a college degree. College graduates generally earn more than non-college graduates, but college does not prohibit one from also training in a trade or vocation. Trade schools offer a quick means to potentially lucrative and in-demand careers. Construction, oil and gas industry, and plumbers are in high demand, along with many other skilled laborers. Air Traffic controllers, a highly lucrative and in high need merely requires as Associate's degree. A business degree would be a great asset to a plumber or electrician with an entrepreneurial mindset. Nonetheless, graduating from college should not be mandatory to have a comfortable life. There was a time when a high school diploma indicated a basic level of literacy and perseverance, as well as nominal skill sets. The Department of Education's National Center for Educational Statistics shows that reading proficiency is "below basic" for 20-28% of high school graduates between the years 1992-2015. Given those numbers, it is sad but not shocking that applicants who are tested for basic office jobs, including sample filing, have a 30% fail rate.

Richard Arum and Josipa Roska's 2010 book, *Academically Adrift*, discusses research involving over 2,300 undergraduates at over 20 colleges. Their findings were that 45% of undergrads demonstrated no significant improvement in skills such as writing, complex reasoning, and critical thinking during their first two years of college. That bears repeating. Almost half of those students did *not* improve in two years of college!

Obviously, there are serious flaws in our system. And thus your involvement as a parent is seriously needed. Whether you choose to work within the system or go outside of it, knowledge of what is happening and a means to work around it will strengthen the educational experience for your children. Merely assuming that a "good" K-12 education and even a "good" college will prepare your child for your vision of independence and success may be a bit of a stretch these days. Assuring, not assuming, that your child is learning and on the path to independence and success is the better choice. We believe your knowledge of how the system works and knowledge of other options can make all the difference.

College and Beyond

One of the many advantages of taking charge of your own education is that it plants a seed of empowerment and a questioning of the status quo. Given the fast-paced lives of our society, in this millennium especially, that is an unquestionably good thing. Rare are the days of starting and ending your career with the same employer and leaving with a hefty retirement package. Capability in areas of creativity, critical thinking, problem solving, and finding new ways to accomplish new and old tasks are the currency of the future. Who best to take on such roles than one who has already questioned the system and found a superior way to build a better mouse-trap, as it were, with their education? One could argue that such a person has a leg up for careers and graduate education. Further, if one earns proficiency and degrees younger than most, they have more time to explore additional education and other experiences, before societal and practical pressures require them to do otherwise. This knowledge will make for a better prepared young adult for our brave new world. Noel's dissertation interviewing radically early college students showed her that participants were happy with the path they chose. No wringing of hands for missing potential quintessential teenage experiences (assuming they did), but gratitude for the freedom to choose the path that best suited them.

Taking the road less traveled is not for the faint of heart. So, as your journey through educational choices continues, options for careers and grad schools may also be a bit off the beaten path as well. As discussed earlier, should you opt for the earlier-than-average school path, you can opt to do the same for graduate school or take time to double, or triple major, or equally take time to earn experience and money. Whether graduate schools and careers value your unique approaches, or not, will be telling as to how creative and open-minded they are. Clichés of "Doogie Howser" and "Sheldon Cooper" may come up, but they are successful individuals with friends, thriving careers, and love in their lives. So, bring it on!

Graduate school applications are the same whether you are a teenager or not. Just like college. Standardized test scores, letters of recommendation, good grades, and demonstrable passion are all needed. Those skill sets are not limited to one age group. Like all college admissions processes, it can be a complex, unfair, and secretive endeavor. Again, many books have been and will continue to be written about admissions. College consultants can be an amazing resource to help winnow the field of options and explain the processes some colleges prefer.

Jobs are being invented and eliminated constantly. Just as there is no longer a thriving whip and buggy transportation market, there will be industries and jobs that fade into oblivion through innovation soon enough. Conversely, those innovations create new markets and beget more jobs. Helping your child embrace their own passions and strengths in a way that best benefits them can be an amazing way to prepare them for this reality.

At its best, a unique educational path allows a student time to pursue their interests for the joy of it, not to merely check off a requisite box in the application process of high school resumes and college applications. The beauty of learning and exploring for its own reward will make for a more whole human. Jumping through hoops with the mindset of, "I'll be happy when...I'm done with finals / I graduate / I land a good job / {fill in your blank}" is a recipe for unhappiness. Joy and passion come from following one's heart. Surely, that is the endgame. Helping your children to become joyful adults in how they feel and how they act in the world.

References

National Center for Education Statistics. (2019). *The Condition of Education 2019*. https://nces.ed.gov/programs/coe/pdf/coe_cnb.pdf.

Looking Back with Nancy: Parenting a Teen in Grad School

When Noel was 16 and considering the Ph.D. program in Educational Psychology for the Gifted and Talented at the University of North Texas, we drove to Denton for her to meet with one of the professors, Dr. Anne Rinn. We agreed that I would stay in the building, but would only be involved in the meeting if Noel decided it appropriate. I sat in the hallway, a ways off from the office. Noel met with Anne. They had a good rapport and the program seemed like it would be a perfect fit given her interests and career plans. Anne asked Noel how she got to Denton, to which Noel replied she and I had made the 3½ drive that morning from College Station. Anne asked if Noel wanted me to meet her. Not wanting to appear that she needed her mommy, nor wanting to appear that she was too cool to have her mother be involved either, she walked the middle ground of deferring that decision to Anne. Anne repeated the question later and Noel again deferred to her. Luckily, Anne wanted to meet me—because I absolutely wanted to meet her!

I thought this was a very perceptive approach from Noel—recognizing that one event can be viewed from a myriad of perspectives, yet knowing that first impressions are critical. I was impressed. Emotional maturity and perceptiveness are difficult things to teach. Like all skill sets, some come more readily than others (Ask Noel how good she is at doing a cartwheel or putting her shoes away).

Life as a grad student vs. undergrad is quite different. Even though she was 16, she was less active in campus life and busy working as a TA (teacher assistant) or RA (research assistant). The academic stresses were easier than learning how to function in an office. When people know of you before you know them, you don't really get the chance to make a first impression; their opinion may already have been formed. This is a reminder, like then, and always, that you can only control your own self and must remember that people have their own issues for which you have little, if any, control. This level of perceptiveness about people and why they did or did not do things was actually one of the ways I first recognized that Noel was gifted as a toddler. Yet that perceptiveness didn't mean she was always cool under pressure or feelings weren't hurt. Growing up comes through experience.

Parenting a teenager is already tough, and when they're in graduate school, it adds a unique challenge. UNT's Toulouse Graduate School considered all its students adults, regardless of their age. Noel was their youngest graduate at 19, and presumably their youngest student when she began at 16. Although she was certainly a mature 16-year old when she started her Ph.D. program, she was still a teenager with age appropriate behavior and mindset some days. Parenting a teen/young adult can be a little tricky, at best. When should you be a sounding board and when should you be the adult with life experience to offer? When to be the parent is equally a subjective judgement call. I received some great advice along the way. Probably my favorite nugget was that a parent starts off as a caregiver, transitions to coach, and then ends up as a consultant. That transition to coach should come around middle school or so, and the transition to consultant, for sure, by college. Yet, age wise she was a junior in high school when she started her Ph.D., so that made things a little trickier. When you are parenting "the road less travelled", there are many decisions made that are extraordinarily subjective and unique.

A foundation of love and respect helped a tremendous amount. A child, no matter their age, should feel like there is an open dialogue with their parents and feel that their parents have their best interest at heart. That foundation can solve many problems. Growing up, making mistakes, and learning from those mistakes is literally how the brain prunes itself to gain wisdom. The styles of bad parenting in the past 20 years which I've seen come into vogue have had great names: "Free range parenting" is a modern day twist on hippie-style parenting with even less involvement. The logic is that children are sentient creatures and should not be burdened with labels and rules by adults. The "Tiger parent" came from the book *Battle Hymn of the Tiger Mother* by Amy Chua, working off the premise that traditional Chinese parents who set strict boundaries are better parents as their culture values good grades and work ethic over self-esteem that Western parents tend to prefer. The "Helicopter parent" speaks to the idea of a parent constantly on top of their children to make sure they are on top of all problems and situations, so as to be connected with and help their kid whenever needed. The latest and worst of these is the "lawnmower parent" mowing down any obstacles or problems before the child even has to deal with them so they never need experience hardship. A parent likely thinks that removing a challenging situation is helping their child. Yet, not allowing a child the requisite experiences of independent problem solving is harmful on an emotional and physiological level. A child will learn to believe they are too incompetent to manage their own lives since Mom or Dad always jump in for them and handle any and all situations. And they have no experience to prove otherwise.

As a mom, my desire to make her unusual path the easiest it could be was strong. It was sheer willpower that stopped me becoming a "helicopter with a razor lawnmower blade attachment" parent. Based on research and the wisdom of others, I knew that there were many challenges she would have to work out on her own. It was usually harder for me to back off than for her to power on. Her Dad and I did the best we could: mistakes were made, triumphs happened anyways. And just like Noel, we have no regrets.

"I got my Ph.D. when I was 19, I don't want to draw anymore, and I think I've earned it!"

Looking Back with Noel: My Dissertation

Writing and defending your dissertation is the final stage of earning a Ph.D. It's something that you are preparing for and thinking about from day one, although the real work doesn't start until you pass your qualifying exams and finish your coursework. By the time I got to that stage, although I was interested in so many different ideas, I knew it was going to go where I had figured it would since that very first day: I needed to research early college.

I already knew at this point that there wasn't much information out there about early college. What I didn't realize that there was *absolutely none* that didn't specifically address early college programs. Early college programs are often residential, associated with specific colleges, and have their own staff and events for students under 18. These are great programs with great results: they offer unrivaled opportunities to talented students. But, the experience is just totally different. Same-age academic peers? Moving away from home, sometimes across the country, for a boarding school experience? Counselors, advisors, and even prom? This was nothing like what I did in my early college journey. I wasn't represented, and anyone else doing what I had done wasn't being represented either. Part of the reason for this was that no one cared about this population, if they even knew it existed. Early college programs are researched primarily by the staff of those same early college programs. I had a unique chance to access this population since I had been through what they had.

Furthermore, research on early college mainly focuses on those who did not do so radically early. Admittedly this makes sense as it is presumably a very small population, but once again these people were being ignored. It seems reasonable to assume that college at 17 is pretty different from college at 15 or college at 13 or college at 11.

By polling various forums, email loops, organizations, and clubs, I was able to recruit ten people for interviews about early college without the use of a program. I promised those people that I would work with their schedule because I was so desperate for numbers (I had no idea how many people had done this, and therefore needed everyone I could get hold of). I kept that promise by conducting an international interview at 1 a.m., which wasn't as bad as you might think.

To attempt to summarize that research would be a bit difficult, as we produced so many fascinating results. But, the most important finding is that these people are happy and healthy and successful. Not all of them are Nobel prize winners or astronauts or something...actually, none of them are as of yet. But they were all generous with their time, fun to talk to, thoughtful and interesting, funny and friendly, and overall satisfied with early college. One of my participants actually didn't need to go to college at all, but was forced to so as to avoid breaking truancy laws. She feels she wouldn't have had any better of a time had she gone when she was older (which, again, she legally could not since she would be a criminal if she did not enroll in school at the time but had completed K-12).

Was it always easy? No, but it was always worth it. It wasn't about being the fastest, or the youngest, or the best (In fact, most of my participants seemed to have a somewhat lackadaisical attitude towards academia, and seemed uninterested in working for a 4.0 in college). It wasn't about attention or media or fame (which, by the way, doesn't make you any money, so I don't know why anyone would choose to seek that out). It was just about doing what needed to be done. Saying people go to college early because they want to be famous is like saying someone got heart surgery to be famous. You get heart surgery because you have some situation that can't be resolved without heart surgery, and as much as you'd love to coexist with the rest of the world without needing heart surgery, that's not an option.

My dissertation was especially satisfying knowing that I was working with a population that was unique and not represented in the academic world. My participants were happy to pay it forward and perhaps dispel the often one-dimensional caricature that such students are either a Sheldon Cooper or a Doogie Howser. For me to be able to laugh with, and connect so easily with, my participants made the hard work easier and more rewarding. Writing this book is part of me paying it forward as I know there are many smarter and more motivated young whippersnappers out there who could benefit from my journey. I also know there are many other students who aren't being served in their school and want something better for themselves too. I didn't get a Ph.D. at 19 for the fun of it, because honestly, it wasn't that much fun, although it certainly had its moments. I got a Ph.D. because I wanted to understand the system better. I am writing this book with the hope of making the system better.

Epilogue

Our goal was to show you that there are many paths to a great education for your kids. Creative approaches, including acceleration and homeschooling have an incredible track record of success. Customizing the education of your children is a far superior option than blindly following the K-12 model provided by the government. Remember that before 1954, the consensus was that no human could run one mile faster than 4 minutes. It was thought the human body was incapable of such a feat. Yet, lo and behold, along comes Roger Bannister, a medical school student, and breaks it with a half second to spare. The heretofore impossible has now been done over 1300 times. Roger Bannister only held that record for 46 days before someone ran it a little faster. Yet despite the analogy, life isn't a race, it is a journey. A common misconception (and harmful, hurtful assumption) about our families is that we pursued early college due to the view of life as a race: we wanted to be done sooner because we wanted to "beat"others, break a record, get press. In truth, we wanted to be done sooner because it's better to be done sooner. We were going at the speed that came naturally to us, and if there's nothing else you take away from reading this book, let it be that you shouldn't feel bad for going at the speed that comes naturally to you.

Don't let assumptions cloud your judgment. What mindset, fear, or obstacle is holding you back?

Now that we're at the end of the book, it may be time to explore the meaning of the title—or it may be past that time, in which case, oh well. An understandable question would be what it actually means to "turn on the power." If empowerment is about awareness and opportunities, then we have sought to provide awareness of issues in modern education as well as opportunities many can pursue without reliance on outside support or approval. If empowerment is something needed especially by the disempowered of the world, then we have offered solutions that benefit women and minorities sometimes even more than they do others. If empowerment is about doing things independently instead of playing by someone's rigged rules…well, there's nothing more independent than leaving traditional education behind, and inversely, nothing more rigged than traditional education!

It's certainly not as straightforward as simply flipping on a light switch; turning on the power—your power—involves first and foremost a change of mindset. An attitude of asking for forgiveness afterwards rather than permission before will undoubtedly get you into some sticky situations, but it may help you dodge so, so many unnecessary struggles. With a child's entire life on the line—where they spend at *least* 18 years (but most likely 22), five days a week, eight-ish hours a day (not including homework or extracurriculars)—there's no point in spending all that time in the dark!

Noel Jett, Ph.D. is currently on the final steps in the process of becoming a Licensed Professional Counselor, intending to focus on the unique counseling needs of the profoundly gifted.

Haley Taylor Schlitz has entered her second year of law school at the Dedman School of Law in Dallas and hopes to use her legal career to defend the rights of students and educators in Texas.

Nancy Shastid works as a paralegal and continues to volunteer with the Texas Parents of the Profoundly Gifted and dedicates her time to gifted families in need of guidance and resources.

Myiesha Taylor, M.D. remains an emergency physician while homeschooling her youngest child, Hana, and facilitating the early college routes of her older children, Ian and Haley.

CPSIA information can be obtained
at www.ICGtesting.com
Printed in the USA
BVHW031020040622
638838BV00002B/8

9 781733 775885